THE

SURVIVAL GUIDE

FOR TODAY'S

CAREER WOMAN

Victoria Rayner

INFO NET PUBLISHING

SAN CLEMENTE, CALIFORNIA

Illustrations by Richard Mandrachio, Vivi Boas

Cover design by Karen Fong

Typographical design
by Robert Biddle of Artefac

Back cover:
Photo by Russ Fischella
Hairstyle by Greg G

Info Net Publishing

P. O. Box 3789

San Clemente, CA 92674

ISBN 0-924272-06-6

THE SURVIVAL GUIDE

FOR TODAY'S

CAREER WOMAN

Dedication

This book is dedicated to the hundreds of women who
I need not name because they know who they are. They took
the time to write, share their stories, and advise me. Without
their outspoken contributions, I would not have learned
so much about the intimate lives of other women.

Table of Contents

Introduction

*W*omen are becoming increasingly vulnerable to mental and physical fatigue as they try to juggle friends, family and career. The daily pressures of life demand that women attempt to cope. In response to chronic emotional strain they become overworked and run down. A destructive cycle slowly evolves; anger, frustration and disillusion develop. Women try to achieve the unattainable: perfection in all areas of their lives. When they fail to meet these unrealistic goals they punish themselves. Their guilt propels them to intensify their commitment and to drive themselves even harder. Physical fatigue, mental irritability, depression and increased illness are all symptoms of professional burnout.

Many women feel at a loss to come up with effective responses and alternative solutions to everyday, anxiety-producing situations. This book is designed to assist the career woman in reducing the apprehension that often accompanies professional and personal success.

A calm disposition, cheerfulness, a sense of wonder and a positive attitude about life are all signs of healthy well-being. Throughout the book there are helpful suggestions to aid the working woman in more effectively responding to stress.

No career woman, even after reading this book, is expected to resolve all her conflicts or release all her tension. The first step toward a better life, however, is self-realization. The success of a professional woman's career and personal life depends on her willingness to probe the depths of her existence without hesitation. The capacity to delight in simple pleasures, to perceive daily activities as interesting and to feel at peace with herself must come from within.

It is time for professional women to assess how their lives are going. There is no virtue in being a victim. Losing balance and giving up control is a ridiculous price to pay for career success, especially since it is not necessary. Women have a natural instinct to create meaning in their lives. This book focuses on how the professional woman can enjoy her life and her career to the fullest without undue sacrifice.

Acknowledgments

I would like to express my gratitude to Richard Mandrachio for his editorial assistance, wisdom, judgment, sound advice and the artwork he contributed to this project.

My appreciation also goes to Jim Weyrauch, vice president of the National Council of Field Labor Locals and president of Local 644 of the American Federation of Government Employees, for all the detailed information he contributed pertaining to sexual harassment in the workplace and facts on working women.

A special thanks to my loving husband, Othmar Stubler, for his tireless patience, and for leaving me alone to struggle with the arduous preparation of this manuscript.

I am profoundly grateful to my good friend, Jude Hanson, whose ideas and enthusiasm made my writing more enjoyable. Her input also has contributed to making this a better book.

Finally, my sincere gratitude goes to Herb Wetenkamp for believing in this project and having the insight to publish this book for working women. To him I am most indebted.

The Survival Guide

for Today's

Career Woman

CHAPTER 1

Coping with Stress

*W*hen we think of stress, many different visions fill our mind. For example, we may picture ourselves stuck on an expressway in congested traffic or we may recall a recent argument with our boss or with our spouse. Perhaps, when we think of stress we are reminded of our fears about our economic future or about the loss of a loved one either through death or divorce. Stress can be brought about by any number of life's common dilemmas.

"Type A" Behavior Patterns

Stress can be defined as any life situation that chronically irritates or aggravates you. Scientific studies indicate that certain personality types are more prone to stress than others. For example, "Type A" personalities—people who are hard-driving, career and success orientated, volatile, and easily excitable—are prime candidates for stress. These individuals are not merely impatient and harried, they spend a disproportionate amount of energy struggling against the normal constraints of time. Such persons have come to live with, accept, and adapt to stress in such a way that they are no longer even aware of its impact on their health or on their psychological well-being.

Today, working women are particularly prone to stress because of all the demands that are placed on them. The popular belief is that women can sustain a successful career and private life without sacrifice. Rewarded for their dedication to hearth and home and often punished for separating from it, many professional women feel they must constantly prove that they can maintain control over both their family life and their professional life. It is not uncommon for women who are seriously overstressed to deny their exhaustion, even to themselves. They have the characteristic of overdoing it. Determined to succeed professionally, they easily become over-involved and over-extended.

For a career woman to get ahead, she must exert an almost superhuman effort just to achieve parity with her male colleagues. Breaking through the "Good Ol' Boy" network to be accepted on equal terms for comparable or superior work can be enormously frustrating. It is no wonder that many women complain of being burned out.

Burnout

It is difficult to determine when the burnout process starts exactly. This is mainly because a highly successful woman will rarely admit that she is having trouble balancing all the different aspects of her life. Out of pride and her compulsion to prove herself, she may try to cope, and in the process, deny her mental exhaustion. Of course, there is a difference between "temporary fatigue" and "total burnout."

Burnout is a slow process that evolves gradually over a long period of time. It occurs when excessive demands are made on an individual by their job, spouse, family, friends, their own value system or by society. Burnout is the depletion of energy, of inner resources and of one's ability to cope with the emotional strains of her life.

You have to really question whether you are a victim of actual burnout or just temporary fatigue. One way to decipher the difference is to examine what affect the constant stress of unrelenting pressure has had on your feelings and perceptions. When a substantial period of rest does not refresh your body and renew your state of mind, you may be a victim of temporary or permanent burnout. In his book, *Woman's Burnout: How To Spot It, How To Reverse It, and How to Prevent It*, Dr. Herbert Freudenberger describes the various stages of burnout as follows: the compulsion to prove, intensity, subtle deprivations, dismissal of conflict and needs, distortion of values, heightened denial, disengagement, observable behavior changes, depersonalization, emptiness, depression, and total burnout exhaustion.

Impact of Stress Upon Health

As you go through your day you encounter a variety of situations. Some are pleasurable for you while others are more difficult and taxing. The way you respond to serious pressures has a major impact upon your physical health. Our bodies are important indicators of our stress levels. Constant worry leads to long-term stress. Chronic stress gradually weakens the immune system and lowers the body's resistance to disease.

Stress is a disease that creates other diseases, according to psychiatrist Ainsley Meares in his book, *Relief Without Drugs*. Studies have shown that as many as 75% of all medical complaints are stress related. Scientists do not yet understand all the ways in which brain chemicals are related to emotion and thoughts. However, what they do know is that the way one thinks has a profound affect upon how well one's body functions as a whole.

Fight-or-Flight Syndrome

Most significantly, stress can increase blood pressure that can lead to heart disease. Whenever you're under severe emotional pressure, your body goes into a state of "red alert." This response is called the "fight-or-flight" syndrome. Certain hormones and other chemicals are released which, in turn, produce an increase in heart rate and perspiration and cause blood pressure to rise. Depending upon the degree of emotional strain, this is what happens to your body in varying intensities.

Each of us has our own individual and recurrent bodily warnings that signal us when we are under too much strain. It may be an ache in the lower back or a pain in our neck or a nagging form of discomfort between our shoulder blades. Anxiety over constant problems can result in tension headaches, various stomach and digestive disorders, and even ulcers.

Stress Affects the Skin and Scalp

Because of close links to the nervous system the skin is very sensitive to emotional distress. Stressful events in our lives can easily trigger negative skin responses resulting in anything from a major outbreak of blemishes to an itchy, red, inflamed rash. Common skin disorders such as herpes (cold sores), psoriasis (red, scaly plaques on elbows, knees and scalp), acne, and dermatitis (redness, blistering, swelling and scaling), are not directly caused by stress, but they are triggered by stress. Subsequently, it has scientifically been proven that emotional turmoil can lead to, or aggravate, problematic medical conditions.

Chronic anxiety also affects the body in other negative ways. Severe dandruff, generalized hair thinning or serious hair loss can occur from long-term exposure to stress. Some people are more susceptible than others to stress related medical problems. According to Dr. Jonathan Zizmor in his book, Super Skin, "Many people who come to the doctor seeking explanations of rashes, eruptions, or hives actually are often suffering from nothing more than stress, tension, and psychological unhappiness."

The Emotional Side Effects of Stress

Stress causes us to feel mentally and physically fatigued. If left untreated it can lead to confusion, feelings of powerlessness and aloneness, waning enthusiasm, lack of motivation, depression, a sense of despair or impeding danger, sudden panic attacks, restlessness, and forgetfulness.

Another common symptom of stress is loss of sexual desire. According to Dr. Kenneth Greenspan in an article on stress in the Ladies' Home Journal, April 1992, "When the body's stress hormones have been put on alert, loss of sexual desire is normal in both animals and humans. This is nature's way of helping us concentrate on escaping from danger."

Life is full of stress; it is unavoidable. Even so-called pleasant events can cause stress. Changes in our life situations such as marriage, relocation, vacation or outstanding personal achievements can cause emotional turmoil and increase our chances of getting physically sick. When we change jobs, houses, or relationships, we need to adjust to our loss and to the new situation. Such adjustments always involve stress, yet if we do not make changes in our routine, we often feel bored and stagnant.

Stress Transference

Not only is our health compromised when we encounter stress but so are our intellectual ability and functioning. When we are under pressure we are not always rational, sensible and pleasant to be with. The effect of stress on our emotions directly influences our relationships with others that we come in contact with.

When there is more work to be done or a deadline hanging over our heads, we try to speed up and work faster. Some of us find it exciting to try to do two or three things at once. When we respond to pressure by rushing, any challenge that gets in our way arouses our furor and we become impatient. As our stress levels mount, we lose our perspective. We often are unreasonable and insensitive to others around us. Our spouses, children, co-workers and employees are bound to get the blunt end of our frustration.

We tend to be more rigid and inflexible when we are "uptight." When our emotional temperature rises, our judgment, productivity and intellect are lowered. Under high stress, women report a series of negative, unmanageable emotions such as the following: anger, cynicism, irritation, the inability to accept criticism, impatience, and intolerance.

Ways to Combat Stress

Many of the conditions that we encounter on a day-to-day basis are stressful. Yet each of us holds the power to control much of the stress we experience in our lives. It was Abraham Lincoln who said, "People are as happy as they make up their minds to be." In fact, researchers have concluded that external circumstances have little effect on psychological well-being. Dr. David G. Meyers writes in his article "Understanding Happiness" (*Health Hotline*, July 1992), "There are four inner traits that foster happiness: a high self-esteem, a sense of personal control, optimism and socializing."

Stress does not always have to be harmful. If we think of stress in positive terms we can use it as a source of motivation. Stress arouses, alerts and activates us. A student undergoing the stress of an exam may achieve levels of intellectual application that far exceed that of his or her normal functioning. This is why it is not necessary to eliminate stress altogether. Women need to manage stress rather than remove it from their lives. The following suggestions will assist you in becoming a more successful stress manager.

30 Proven Ways to Manage Stress

1. Break free from your everyday routine by viewing problems in your daily life in a more creative way. Exploit stress by using it as an opportunity to learn and develop new, life-enhancing skills. Whenever possible use your imagination to find a different approach to cope with some unpleasant situation or work activity.

2. Be more aware of the ironies of everyday life and cultivate a good sense of humor. Learn to laugh at life.

3. Stop depriving yourself of emotional pleasures; you need them to refresh your spirit.

4. Be careful not to overextend your energy. Pay more attention to your inner clock. Learn to pace yourself. Take more time out for relaxation. Feeling relaxed and in control goes hand-in-hand with a strong, active immune response.

5. Honor your special skills and abilities. Give yourself credit and reward yourself when you accomplish something.

6. Eat properly. Eating the right foods will help you to think and feel better.

7. Exercise clears the mind and helps us to let off steam. Participate two to three times per week in a vigorous exercise routine. When our bodies are in good physical condition, we are better prepared for stressful situations.

8. Expand your social life. Plan and spend more time with friends and loved ones who offer support.

9. When performing tasks, slow down. You can be a slave to time or it's master. By slowing down you can study a situation more thoroughly. You can evaluate any problems that may arise and, in turn, consider a variety of solutions. A slower pace means less time required to re-do.

10. Be more spontaneous. One of the reasons children are so energetic is that they do things for the sheer thrill and delight of it. Try new things. Make your journey through life an adventure. Strive to discover something new every day.

11. Rest and replenish your energy. Not every minute must be accounted for. Give yourself permission occasionally to waste time. Let yourself become distracted and amazed by your immediate environment.

12. Take time to find and participate in activities you enjoy. Create a "play sheet." List as many things as you can think of that you have always wanted, imagined, or fantasized about doing. Perhaps what you would like to do is to go sailing, take a cooking course, attend a concert, see a play, participate in a sports activity or create music. Start off by picking one playful activity from the list and simply go do it! Experience how great it makes you feel.

13. Loosen your need for control when you find yourself becoming overburdened … Delegate!

14. When you are under stress, be sure to take extra, special care of yourself. Spend some time on your personal appearance. Have your hair styled or get your nails done. Better yet, get both a manicure and pedicure.

15. Allow yourself the privilege of making new mistakes. No one is perfect. Give yourself permission to be wrong occasionally. Stop setting rigid, grueling standards for yourself. Stop battering yourself and show some compassion.

16. Listen to your personal dialogue. What negative messages are you constantly repeating in your mind? Use affirmations to strengthen your "self-talk." Write down a series of one-sentence supportive statements that will remind you of your strengths. Keep them handy by carrying them in your wallet or placing them on your visor in your car. View them at different intervals throughout the day.

17. Take care of your health. When you are under severe stress see a medical doctor for a complete check-up.

18. If you're under pressure, avoid people who have colds. Remember, your immune system is already compromised.

19. During extreme periods of stress, avoid smoking and eliminate alcohol and caffeine consumption entirely.

20. When you encounter a particularly stressful situation, record your thoughts about your experience in writing. Try to pinpoint when you first started to feel pressured, overwhelmed and fatigued. This will help diminish some of your anxiety so you can explore what promotes these stressful situations.

21. Try to change the circumstances that are causing stress in your life. Assess what unpleasant conditions you can restructure or ultimately eliminate.

22. Set short- and long-term goals to improve your situation. Start by separating your needs from your desires. Focus on what things are truly essential to you and will bring you peace of mind.

23. Take time to relate better to co-workers or associates. We can accomplish much more and with less stress when we can count on the help and support of those we work with.

24. Focus on your needs versus the desires of others. Overcome indecisiveness and learn to say, "No." Take time to consider the consequences of your choices before accepting a request from your spouse, a companion or a colleague.

25. Enjoy your every day experiences more fully. Make every moment in your life count. Be aware of the small miracles in life.

26. Engage in sexual or intimate involvement. It will help you to feel calm and less stressed and to gain a better perspective.

27. Prepare yourself for situations that may be potentially stressful. Focus on what you must do. Rehearse in your mind how your going to go about handling the situation. As you mentally walk yourself through it, use positive self-talk if you feel yourself becoming overwhelmed.

28. Read literature on anxiety, stress and burn-out.

29. Seek professional counseling if symptoms persist. Schedule an appointment with a psychologist, psychiatrist or social worker.

30. Adopt a healthy philosophy of life. Much of what we experience as stress on a daily basis cannot be changed but our reaction to the stress can be. By making the things we do as pleasurable as possible we improve the quality of our life, which automatically reduces daily tension.

CHAPTER 2

Solving Everyday Problems

roublesome situations come upon us gradually. They have a habit of growing out of control and of affecting our lives in a million indirect ways. When we are gripped by difficulties, everyday life can seem unbearable. Problems change our whole pattern of thinking. Negative thoughts throw our personalitities out of balance and cause us to experience anxiety that manifests itself in moodiness, irritability, nervousness and restlessness. Excessive behavior is based on emotional imbalance. Overindulging in food, alchohol and drugs are direct results of unbalanced emotional patterns.

Happiness and contentment cannot penetrate our minds when we are tormented. In an effort to escape reality and to repress pain, we screen out many uncomfortable experiences. We often permit too much time to pass before we attend to our problems. Then, before we know it, we find ourselves completely submerged in a full-blown crisis. Denial is a common psychological defense that clouds our thoughts and prevents us from putting our situation into proper perspective. Running away from our problems is not really the answer. We cannot completely detach ourselves from our difficulties. Inevitably, we are brought to the realization that our lives are a reflection of our decisions, both conscious and unconscious. When we lose control of our problems, we automatically lose control over our lives. Both success and happiness depend upon our abiltiy to deal with problems.

Many women, however intelligent, can misunderstand the nature of trouble. Our worries pose a very real danger to our mental and physical health. A problem that goes on too long can engulf us with depression. The mental and emotional strain of being constantly confronted with an unresolved dilemma can result in paying a serious price in our health and mental well-being.

Sometimes, we are so reluctant to deal with a challenging circumstance that we wait until the situation reaches crisis proportions.

Then, we are forced to act. It's hard to make intelligent decisions when nervous and apprehensive. Although some of us claim to function better under pressure, such conditions make it impossible to view situations objectively. This is especially true when emotions gain control over behavior. The following chapter will provide ways in which women can solve simple or critical problems by devising practical solutions with little or no difficulty.

Passive Behavior

No matter how much we wish it weren't true, problems are unavoidable in life. Regardless of our age, wealth or position, we all have our share of them. Some troubles are attendant upon the very act of living. In fact, it is said that a certain amount of disquietude is essential to good, robust living. Most of us need difficulites and conflicts if we are to mature and face our weaknesses. Problems prevent us from becoming too complacent. It is only when problematic situations get out of hand, when we give them the power to crush our spirits, that we are in trouble and should be concerned.

Chronic troubles are problems that we go around but never get past. They are considered more significant because they result in a long series of frustrations that can cause inner turmoil. Problems, when left unattended, can pervert our personality, distort our natural instincts and make us nervous and high-strung. Most of the pressure in our lives can be dealt with if only we would face our problems head on, with firmness and conviction. However, most of us run scared and haven't the courage. Moreover, we do not take the time to confront all the individuals or situations that are causing conflict in our lives. The reason for this neglect is not hard to understand. In fact, there are a multitude of explanations as to why we may refuse to deal directly with our problems. The most common of all is fear.

All too often, fear prevents us from taking action and from doing what we really want to do about our problems. Fear is often based upon irrational beliefs. It can be brought about by real or imagined future events. Many of the bad things that we perceive may never happen but when we are apprehensive, we are sure they will. What actually does occur, however, is not as important as our perception of what happens. Fear requires no proof to be believed. It is a destructive mental habit. It inhibits assertive behavior by breaking down our self-assurance until we lack the very confidence we need to take the necessary action to solve our predicament. It causes us to panic; we become emotionally paralyzed and function far below the level of our capabilities. Fear is a handicap that keeps us from getting what we really want out of life. To conquer fear, we must fight the urge to avoid it. We must directly confront our anxiety. It is the only way that we can help to reduce it. We must teach ourselves to plan ahead instead of worrying ahead.

Indecision also inhibits us and leaves us paralyzed, preventing us from taking action. It can result in endless procrastination that makes us feel helpless and locked into our difficulties. The way we handle our problems can reveal our intellectual strengths and weaknesses to those around us. By refusing to confront a problem, we are making a choice to give up our freedom. If we let others make our decisions for us, we end up with a sense that our lives are not really our own. When we lack the initiative to solve our own problems, we often find that well-intentioned friends and family members will frequently try to push us into handling situations the way they see fit. However, this well-intended but unhelpful advice does little to rectify our situation. By putting others in charge of our problems, we are under the false assumption that if anything goes wrong, they will be our scapegoats. But, everyone has their own agenda. Most of the time, the motives of others are quite different from those of our own. Many-a-person has sworn undying loyalty, only to turn on us in order to save his or her own neck.

Placing our problems in the hands of others can only complicate matters. In the end, we are still accountable for our choices and must bear the burden of the consequences. By avoiding issues, by deferring to others, or by waiting for situations to magically resolve themselves, we relinquish control and invite chaos. If the problem escalates because of the involvement of others (which it generally does), we often experience anxiety and guilt for not having handled our own affairs to begin with. We could also end up resenting the help we have been given because our own sense of importance is diminished by the efforts of others. Taking voluntary control over our problems and trying to work them out before someone else's solutions are forced upon us will give us a sense of inner fulfillment and will boost our self-esteem.

Motivation

How successful you will be in solving any prolem will depend on three factors: how badly you want to rectify the situation, how hard you are willing to work at achieving a resolution and how persistent you are.

As Calvin Coolidge once said, "Nothing in the world can take the place of persistence. Talent will not; nothing is more common than unsuccessful people with talent. Education will not; the world is full of educated derelicts. Persistence and determination alone are omnipotent. The slogan 'press on' has solved and always will solve problems of the human race."

To solve any difficulty, you must come to terms with the following issues: You are not a victim of sources out of your control. You are not helpless. You do hold the power to make changes in your life. You are capable of dealing with difficulites. You know you will benefit and grow from the experience, regardless of the outcome of your decisions.

Life is hard. It can, in fact, be a struggle. What you do can make a difference. Don't let unexpected changes overwhelm you. Give yourself some credit. You will know what to do; if you don't you will learn. Be flexible; change is an essential ingredient to the growth process.

Problem-Solving Formula

There is a very simple, three-step formula I developed that you can use which will help you to overcome indeciveness and make it easier to decide how to handle problems. The following formula is a well-thought-out plan with carefully defined goals and priorities.

Step 1. When facing a significant problem, the first step is awareness. In order to respond to a problem, not just react to it, we need to understand what is really going on. Some of us become so engrossed in our problems that we simply cannot allow ourselves to see the truth. The more emotional we are about a situation and the stronger we feel about it, the more likely we are to let our feeling substitute for rational thinking. If we are harboring faulty perceptions about our troubles, we cannot possibly come up with sound solutions to correct them.

Before we can rectify an impossible situation, we must first be able to evaluate it with a clear head. Most people find that it is self-defeating to tackle all of their problems at once. They become confused and frustrated. Confront only one problem at a time, starting with the one you feel is the most urgent. Give yourself ample time to obtain all the necessary information you'll need to get to the root of the problem. Closely examine the details surrounding your dilemma by sifting through the relevant facts and by separating them from the irrelevant facts. This process will help you to organize your thoughts.

Step 2. The second step of the problem-solving process is to concentrate on possible solutions rather than on the problem itself. Psychologists claim that most things are accomplished by choice and that choice produces results. However, it is up to each of us to

choose what we really want. There are four basic psychological needs that all of us have:
- the desire for safety, comfort and security
- the desire to love and be loved
- a strong sense of self-worth
- the need for diversity

It is upon these four basic requirements that we base the majority of our decisions.

Find a time and a place where you can relax without interruption. The calmer and more focused you are, the more creative you are likely to be. Start by asking yourself what you can immediately do to simplify your dilemma. Move from short-range approaches to long-range solutions. Consider as many possible alternatives to your predicatment as you can and write them all down.

If your dilemma seems overwhelming, break it down into manageable fractions. This will make it easier to manipulate. Attend to the most urgent aspects of the problem by first dividing it up and writing down sub-solutions. Focus on each segment until you have addressed all facets of the problem. Next, examine the cost and the benefits of each alternative by writing out its "pros" and "cons." This process will help you to examine your options more critically. Discard the unrealistic or unworkable possibilities and you will be left with only the choices that will bring you the most favorable gains.

Some problems are more complicated than others and require additional time and effort to work through. If you find yourself working on a specific problem for a long time without results, you may have become too fatigued to come up with any intelligent solutions. Take a rest and step back from the problem temporarily. Give yourself time to clear your mind. When you attempt to solve the problem again, you will have a fresh, new viewpoint.

Avoid making serious decisions if tired, in poor health, under a lot of stress, angry or depressed. When we are upset our judgment is seriously imparied. Don't limit the time frame for resovling serious issues because you feel pressured.

Once you have made your final decision, ask yourself the following questions: "Is the solution I have chosen emotionally right for me?" "What needs will this solution satisfy in my life?" "Am I willing to accept what goes along with this solution?"

Step 3. The third step involves the willingness to deal with the consequences of your proposed resolution. To be an effective problem-solver, you must conquer the fear of making a mistake. With every decision comes the very real possibility that we could be criticized, be punished or that we could fail. Living through the temporary agony caused by a bad decision is not nearly as devastating as being immobilized by unfounded, pessimistic fears. Know and accept your limitations. Often, we look back at some of the worst mistakes we have made. We find that, as a consequence of those mistakes, we have achieved significant personal growth.

The problem-solving process also involved independent thinking and relinquishing the need for approval by others. Whenever you are confronted with making a decision to solve a problem, whatever it may be, you risk becoming unpopular. Each of us has our own personal values and private reasons for making the choices we make. We must respect our decisions and learn to live with the outcome of our choices. Each of us has an inner wisdom, a voice that tells us what we should and should not do. If you have delayed in making a decision because you are concerned about what other people will say or how they will react, write down any of these worries. On that same paper write down what your conscience tells you to do. Be true to your feelings.

Sometimes our desire for applause interferes with logic and good reason in making choices. Be careful not to let "being liked" become the central point of your decisions. Learn to stand behind your resolutions. There is a big difference between being well-liked and being well-respected. Risk incurring disapproval by taking full responsibility for your own decisions. Whether you realize it or not, you control the attitudes of those around you by your attitude. If you set the stage for others to criticize your decisions, then you can't expect them to support you. By letting go of your desire to please others, you'll find that you will begin to feel more confident. Confidence breeds confidence.

Learn to Be Flexible

It is virtually impossible to predict with complete certainty what the future holds. Just because we have made a decision does not mean we have to be totally committed to it. We should always be prepared to change our position if the situation warrants it. Do not be afraid to contradict yourself if you find yourself facing a situation contradictory to your usual values. Be less concerned about being consistent and more concerned about doing what you feel is right. Never make a concession that forces you to sacrifice your basic principles.

Learn to Say 'No'

One of the best ways to avoid potential problems is to be less compliant. A lot of women feel very guilty when they have to say "no" to someone, especially someone who is important to them. They spend their entire lives trying to please others. If a request becomes an imposition, it infringes upon your basic right not to compromise yourself. There is no virtue in fulfilling a requst unless you can offer your assistance on a truly cooperative basis. If we concentrate too much on the comforts of others at our own expense, we become martyrs. Furthermore, others will come to expect our assistance. Many acts of unselfishness can end in conflict when the burden of self-sacrifice leads to overwhelming resentment. When you are prompted to perform a kind act, do so with your heart. If you must refuse a request, be firm.

Seeking Professional Help

You must remember that no situation is ever hopeless. No matter how bad it may seem, there are usually more resources available than are immediately apparent. If you come up against a problem that requires more background information for a solution, consider attending a workshop or seminar. You can also "brainstorm" with others who can be objective and offer you plausible alternatives. Joining a self-help group will put you into contact with people who are trying to work through problems similar to yours. You can really benefit by listening to the hardships of others and to the problem-solving strategies that they have used to successfully combat their difficulties. Members of a self-help group will hear you out, broaden your view of a predicament and provide you with an entirely new perspective of your world. Quite a few people report that this valuable feedback helps them to resolve their dilemmas.

There can be times when we are overwhelmed by a personal crisis. It may feel as if we are not in control; coping with our situation seems beyond us. These are times when we require more than what we can accomplish alone. We need to look for outside professional help to make the difference. A recent report issued by the National Institute of Health stated that one out of every twelve people suffer, at least once, from serious debilitating depression.

A highly qualified professional will not try to treat you. Instead, he or she will try to educate you by providing you with the necessary information and skills to work through your problems and to function independently. To find a good therapist, contact your local university or ask for a referral from your physician. You also may be able to find a counseling clinic connected with a church or a hospital. You do not have to be a prisoner to your problems if you choose not to be.

Women in the Workplace

*T*he amount of women entering the work force has vastly increased over the past two decades. No longer confined only to the housewife and mother roles, women are showing up in places where they have rarely been observed before. According to the Women's Bureau of the U.S. Department of Labor, "Women now comprise almost 46% of the labor force and account for two out of every three new workers." Several studies indicate that, today, women are committing to lifelong involvement in the labor force and are remaining in the labor market over an extended period of time rather than working intermittently. As a result, women are now choosing employment options that pay well or that have good opportunities for promotion. As women achieve status by actualizing their potential and securing positions of influence, the balance of power between the sexes is slowly and undeniably shifting.

Even though women are filling a wider range of occupations than ever before (many are now becoming bankers and stockbrokers, lawyers and legislators, scientists and doctors), it is unrealistic to think that gender issues related to work will end at any time soon. Despite the fact that most career women yearn to make significant contributions and to be recognized for them, their participation in the work force has only just begun to match that of their male peers. Unfortunately, women's work experiences and the opportunities available to them are still very different.

How Men and Women Differ in the Workplace

Times have changed. Thirty to forty years ago, a man was identified by his job and a woman was identified by what her husband did for a living. Today, however, business has become the central focus in the lives of both men and women.

Studies indicate that men and women handle business differently. Many of these differences can be attributed to early social conditioning. Culturally, men have been programmed to compensate for their weaknesses; women, for their strengths. Sex-role differences are initially taught to us as children by our parents and teachers. As young women mature, they are told it is not ladylike to exert themselves forcefully because power is a masculine trait. Words and phrases that define what is considered as "appropriate male and female behavior" are reinforced throughout adult life by those in authority and by the mass media. Men, women are cautioned, have a certain manner that should not be duplicated by the opposite sex. The most evident reminder that these fixed attitudes still exist is a long-standing joke of the workplace that points out the various ways in which to distinguish a businessman from a businesswomen: It is said that a businessman is aggressive whereas a businesswoman is pushy; he is careful about details, she is picky; he is firm, she is stubborn; he follows through, she doesn't know when to quit; he makes wise judgments and she reveals her prejudices.

In order for women to achieve parity with men in the workplace, women must learn not to undermine their own credibility. They must appear to be competent, confident individuals ... and they will have to project that image. They must not act, dress, talk, walk, think or function in a manner similar to men. Women can bring fresh ideas and changes to the workplace. They have their own unique style and their own way of facing problems, challenges, and victories. For women, the key to success in business is not to imitate professional male behavior. Instead, they need to closely examine men's actions, their successes as well as their failures, and to learn from them. It is counterproductive for women to behave like men because the hierarchy they want to change is devised and regulated by men. Although men are more visible and are presently enjoying the higher status in the workplace, women will continue to prove themselves and to overcome many of the problems that could possibly interfere with the success of their careers.

Male and Female Earnings

Despite the transformation of roles, women are still battling over equal pay for equal work. As women strive to achieve equality in the workplace, the wages that measure their progress move slowly. It is a well-documented fact that there is a gap between men's and women's earnings. A recent study of the career progressions of over one thousand male and female managers in twenty "Fortune 500" companies by researchers at Loyola University of Chicago and Kellogg Graduate School of Management found that, while these two groups were alike in almost every way, the "women with equal or better education earn less on average than men and there are proportionately fewer women in top management positions." The comparable worth controversy is an indication of the nature of the labor market, the possibilities it offers women and the opportunities it restricts.

Pay discrimination, because of an individual's sex, is illegal. The Equal Pay Act states that employers must pay equal wages within their establishment to men and women doing equal work on jobs requiring equal skill, effort and responsibility, which are performed under similar working conditions. The law applies to all wages related to employment payments; this includes overtime, uniforms, travel, and other fringe benefits. If you suspect that you are not receiving equal pay for equal work, you may file a complaint with the Equal Employment Opportunity Commission (EEOC), which enforces the Equal Pay Act. If you prefer, your identity will not be revealed during an investigation of an alleged equal pay violation. For more information, write: U.S. Equal Employment Opportunity Commission, Office of Communications and Legislative Affairs, Washington, DC 20507.

Job Rights

Every career woman should be more aware of her legal job rights. Setting out to learn about your rights as they pertain to job recruitment, training opportunities, working conditions, performance reviews and promotions, is more than just an assertive act. This is especially true when you consider how women, throughout history, have been forced to accept the policies of companies which have notoriously favored male workers. Although there has been progress in the advancement of qualified women into mid- and senior-level management positions, their success stories remain the exception, not the rule. This point is supported by a recent survey of 400 female managers conducted by *Business Week*. Seventy per cent of the women polled believe the male-dominated, corporate culture to be an obstacle to their success.

Many of your rights are protected by federal employment laws and regulations. Similar laws at the state level operate in partnership with federal legislation. Title VII of the Civil Rights Act of 1964 protects workers against discrimination on the basis of sex in most on-the-job aspects of employment. Employers must recruit, train, and promote persons in all job classifications without discrimination. *Every Employee's Guide to Law*, a book by Lewin G. Joel III (Pantheon Press, New York, NY.), is a must for every career woman. It offers information about coping with on-the-job problems, severance pay, workers' compensation and what to do if you're disciplined or dismissed.

Breaking the Glass Ceiling

According to the U.S. Department of Labor's *Pipelines Of Progress*, "Over 50% of the workforce is made up of minorities and women, yet it appears that their advancement is oftentimes hindered by artificial barriers—glass ceilings. The message of this report is very clear. While progress has been made in the workplace by women, the commitment and actions that led to this progress must be maintained and enhanced if the goal of full and equal opportunity is to be realized." The Department of Labor is prepared to assist women to ensure that their job rights are not overlooked when promotional opportunities occur. Although the Department of Labor will firmly and fairly enforce the laws, women must also take personal responsibility for their own career progress. They can accomplish this by identifying jobs with high potential, qualifying themselves, filling entry-level management positions and tracking their progress.

Pregnancy Discrimination

According to the Bureau of Labor Statistics, the number of births in the United States has risen from 3.8 million in 1987 to an estimated 4.2 million in 1990. This is the highest increase since the end of the "baby-boom" years following World War II. The fastest growing segment of the population entering the labor force today are woman of childbearing age. Unfortunately, this seems to have been of very little concern to the business community. Neither American society nor American businesses have acknowledged this reality. If you are considering having a baby, know your rights!

The Pregnancy Discrimination Act (PDA) of 1978 specifically prohibits discrimination because of pregnancy; employers can not refuse to employ a woman in this condition. Neither can they terminate her, force her to go on leave at an arbitrary point during pregnancy, nor can they deny her reinstatement rights due to pregnancy (including credit for previous service, accrued retirement benefits, and accumulated seniority).

The PDA of 1978 requires employers to treat women "disabled" by pregnancy and related conditions in the same fashion as they would treat employees with other health problems that interfere with their ability to work. To obtain more information about your job rights under Title VII, write to the U.S. Equal Employment Opportunity Commission, Office of Communications and Legislative Affairs, Washington, DC 20507.

Maternity and Parental Leave

State maternity and parental leave laws provide for a specific number of weeks that a parent may take off for the birth or the adoption of a child. State family leave laws vary widely. If you have any questions on the law, you should contact your state department of labor, or human and civil rights agencies.

Sexual Harassment On The Job

Sexual harassment takes place when employment decisions affecting an individual (such as hiring, firing, promotions, awards, transfers, or disciplinary action) result from compliance to, or refusal of, unwelcome sexual conduct, according to Title VII of the 1964 Civil Rights Act, as amended in 1972. It is considered sexual harassment for a supervisor to encourage or to force an employee into a sexual relationship and, on the basis of that relationship, compensate the employee with a promotion. It is also sexual harassment for a supervisor to discipline or to deny a promotion to an employee because he or she has rejected sexual overtures.

Sexual harassment is also considered to be any activity that creates an adverse or disagreeable working environment for members of one gender. Such an activity could be carried out by either a supervisor or a co-worker. It could include such actions as the posting of sexually explicit materials, telling sexually oriented jokes, making vulgar remarks, engaging in inappropriate and sexually offensive talk, unwanted sexual teasing or advances, unwelcome touching or rubbing oneself sexually around another person, pressuring employees for dates, receiving unwanted letters, telephone calls, or materials of a sexual nature.

Sexual harassment is more common than most of us think. A survey of over nine thousand federal employees by the Merit Systems Protection Board, a court of appeals for federal employees who have undergone an adverse action, found that 42% of the women who responded had received unwanted sexual attention.

Women have a right to work in an environment that is free of sexual harassment. However, along with that right, they also have the responsibility not to sexually harass other employees. Women need to stop and question their own behavior in order to determine if their own actions are extraneous. According to the Equal Employment Opportunity Commission, the following behavior is considered inappropriate in the workplace: touching or hugging others, giving neck massages, giving personal gifts, asking questions about other employees' personal lives, telling sexy jokes, using sexual innuendoes, making sexual remarks about a person's clothing, anatomy, or looks, or constantly asking a person out.

Stopping Sexual Harassment

Sexual harassment is a legal issue. It is an unlawful practice under Title VII of the Civil Rights Act of 1964, as amended. If you are a victim of sexual harassment, take care to document incidents to support your claim. Write out a description of the behavior and the date and time during which it occurred. Often, the best strategy is to immediately confront the harasser and to persuade him to stop. If this maneuver proves unsuccessful, you can notify your supervisor in writing. Include a warning that if the unwelcome behavior continues, you will take further action. Sign the letter and make two copies. Keep one copy for your records and give the other one to the harasser in front of a witness. If it is your supervisor who is doing the sexual harassment, talk with his supervisor. If your request is not taken seriously, contact the resource department of your company and file a formal complaint. Then, if these actions do not produce a satisfactory response, you can contact the Equal Employment Opportunity Commission (1-800-699-EEOC) for assistance in filing a sex discrimination complaint. Charges of sexual harassment are reviewed by the legal staff as soon as they are filed. Also, you have the option of filing a suit under state laws that protect you against assault, battery, intentional infliction of emotional distress, or intentional interference with an employment contract.

Performance Reviews

Almost all organizations now make use of some type of ratings form as a legal safety net to protect them from wrongful termination claims filed by their ex-employees. Performance reviews are written, detailed reports that examine and assess an employee's progress, their failings as well as their accomplishments. Generally, performance evaluations are prepared and given by a manager or by a supervisor. In most corporations, employees are evaluated every six to twelve months.

Most employees approach their performance review with apprehension. But, the good news is that these reviews can set the stage for more than just an opportunity to defend one's actions. If approached in the right manner, a review can open the door to career advancement. If you spend your evaluation time wisely, you can use it to improve your relations with your boss, to increase his/her willingness to provide needed training, or to request a long-overdue salary increase.

Reviewers generally focus on three major areas: self-appraisal (an employee's own assessment of their strengths and weaknesses), professional areas that need improvement, and future career goals. The best way to make the most of your performance evaluation, and to have some sense of control, is to plan for your review in advance. Ask co-workers how their appraisals had been conducted so that you will know what to expect. Anticipate what you are likely to hear and be ready to respond to possible criticisms. You will probably be required to give either a written or a verbal review of your job performance. So prepare to present your boss with an enumeration of your skills and professional accomplishments. Write out, in advance, any questions you wish to ask or any comments you want to make.

The successful outcome of your review will depend upon the approach you take. After the exchange of pleasantries, encourage your manager to start talking. First, ask what he or she likes the best and the least about your job performance. Listen carefully to what is said without commenting. Concentrate on your boss's tone as well as his or her words. Be aware of any indirect criticisms. Watch for both positive and negative body language. Remain silent until you are asked for your opinion on what has been said. Start your conversation off by acknowledging whatever deficiencies your manager may have pointed out.

Be prepared to admit your shortcomings. Avoid appearing tense, irritated or worried. In a confident tone, clarify the measures you have already taken to alter your behavior or to reverse an unacceptable situation. You may wish to ask your boss for suggestions on how to solve certain problems, but you should have a clear idea of your skills and know your worth to the company.

When your reviewer begins to talk, use receptive body language to express interest. Help your reviewer to feel more comfortable in your presence by maintaining direct eye contact and nodding your head to show you are listening. Keep your arms and legs uncrossed, and smile occasionally to signify friendliness.

The second part of the review process allows you the opportunity to define the quality of your work, the volume of work you have handled, the amount of extra time you have spent on it and the way in which you have attended to the fine details of your job. Emphasize the specific contributions you have made and clearly define how you want to advance in job responsibility. State concrete reasons why you feel you deserve to have a raise or to be promoted. Convince your manager that if you were to receive a pay increase or a promotion, it would benefit the corporation as well as his or her own career plans. Then, go on to explain how.

Few things can trigger dissension more than the feeling of being cheated. If management denies you a salary increase or a promotion, don't let your disappointment or anger show. Instead, make the most efficient use of your review time by pursuing further negotiations. Unless you sense intensely negative vibrations, mention other alternatives to a promotion or to a salary increase. Such additional "perks" are: extended vacation time, business travel, a larger entertainment allowance, a company car, extra insurance coverage, a bonus, flextime or job-sharing.

Flextime

Flextime allows employees to work their allotted number of hours but permits them flexibility in their arrival and departure times. Organizations that offer flextime allow their employees to select their starting and departing times in accordance with their own wishes and individual circumstances. According to the U.S. Civil Service Commission, organizations that utilize flextime report the following advantages: better morale, reduction in short term absences (due to the fact that employees can take care of personal affairs during flexible off-hours), and increased productivity. Furthermore, service hours for the company can be extended and tardiness can be eliminated because the employees select their own starting time.

Employees also benefit from flextime in a variety of ways. First of all, they are more productive because they can adjust their work hours to their own natural body rhythms. Employees can also avoid heavy traffic by missing peak commute hours, hence their traveling time to and from work can be reduced. Most importantly, workers can participate in more family, social and community activities.

Job Sharing

Very few woman can choose to stay at home and take care of their children all day. According to a Ford Foundation study, it is estimated that three out of every four mothers must work full or part-time out of financial necessity. This research indicates that working mothers are now faced with finding solutions to childcare on their own. Restructured jobs that offer more flexible working hours would allow working mothers to stay employed and yet maintain family obligations.

"Job sharing," or "job splitting," is an adaptable work arrangement that involves two people jointly fulfilling the responsibilities of one full-time position. The concept of job sharing is more widely accepted at the present time than it was a few years ago. The benefits to an employer are less absenteeism, less turnover, peak period coverage, the availability of a wider range of skills for a particular job and more employee productivity and efficiency. Whether or not your employer will be receptive to job sharing will depend upon the following issues: your value to the company or organization; your presentation of a solid and legitimate case to withstand the management's misgivings, challenges and questions; finding qualified job-sharing partners; and your plan regarding the division of job responsibilities.

Before you can introduce the concept of job sharing to your employer, you will have to investigate the following: your company's policy regarding inclusion of part-time employees; if there will be an additional cost to your employer to add personnel to the payroll; how job sharing will affect your company benefits; and if you are under contract with a union, whether or not you can still count on their support.

Before approaching your employer and presenting your request, have all of your arguments and answers on hand in the form of a written proposal. It should indicate the following:

1. Background information on job sharing (include in your proposal some examples of where it has been tried).

2. A list of the advantages.

3. A proposed work plan and schedule.

4. Possible suggestions for handling fringe benefits.

5. Any other considerations pertaining to your particular circumstances.

Another new concept to explore is telecommuting, which allows employees to work at home—or in a satellite facility—to complete their work load by interfacing with headquarter computer hookups.

For more information on job sharing and for a list of the states participating and testing job sharing with state employees, contact: New Ways to Work Job Sharing Project, 149 Ninth St., San Francisco, CA 94103 (415) 552-2949.

Changing Jobs

Lifelong career employment is fast becoming an anachronism. According to a 1992 study by Harvard economist James Medoff, job security is increasingly rare these days. Studies indicate that one out of every five Americans was unemployed in 1992 and that white collar workers accounted for 33 percent of the jobless.

William Morin, chairman of one of the nation's largest career-guidance firms, says, "College graduates entering the job market today should expect to make as many as six to seven job changes during the span of their careers." One of the potential drawbacks of changing jobs is the loss of benefits (vacation time, retirement benefits and profit sharing plans). Take charge of your financial future by investigating Individual Retirement Accounts (IRAs), Certificates of Deposit (CDs), or other financial vehicles to assist you in funding your retirement. According to Harvard's Medoff, since 1988 thirty thousand companies have terminated their pension plans. Check with your life insurance agent or your bank for more information on establishing your own benefit and retirement package.

Defining Your Professional Services

When you have learned all that is possible and you find that your work is no longer stimulating, you may wish to explore new career opportunities that are more challenging. As you advance in your chosen field, you acquire expertise and become a far different person than when your career first began. You may find areas of employment open to you now that had not been open to you before. To support a claim that you are qualified for advancement, you will need to record information that indicates the various duties you have performed, the professional skills you have mastered, and the new responsibilities you've handled. Constantly document your achievements in a weekly log. Cite your accomplishments. Keeping a record of your attributes and skills gives you the ammunition to explore the option of extending the boundaries of your existing position. Should an unexpected opportunity arise, by being prepared you will be able to present your job skills at a moment's notice. If your suggested proposal for advancement is refused, you might consider seeking employment elsewhere.

The secret of success is to work smarter, not harder. Research, study and plan your career. Take the initiative and never assume that your boss knows you are doing a good job. Keep your superiors up to date on your progress by organizing and presenting your accomplishments effectively. You never know when the opportunity for a promotion may arise; it would be tragic if you had the necessary qualifications but were unprepared to present them.

Overnight Resume by Donald Asher (Ten Speed Press, P.O. Box 7123, Berkeley, CA. 94707) will provide you with everything you need in order to have your resume ready tomorrow. In his book, Asher, the president of Resume Righters, teaches you the rules of resume writing, how to mask dates without lying and the differences between East Coast and West Coast styles. *Overnight Resume* includes special sections on job search protocol, types of resumes (financial, legal, academic, medical, computer and technical) and gives tips for applying with overseas companies. Another great step-by-step guide for writing resumes is Kim Marino's *The Resume Guide For Women in the '90s* (Ten Speed Press). It is an excellent resource for housewives and moms who are re-entering the job market.

Switching Careers

The role of your career in your life is an important one because most of us spend over half of our waking lives at work. Yet, recent studies reveal that more than 80% of all working people are unhappy at what they are doing to support themselves. There is nothing more frustrating and unbearable than being mismatched with your job. Working at an enjoyable job does not have to be a fantasy; it can be a reality within the grasp of all who choose to reach for it. You should consider switching careers if you are clearly not finding your current career satisfying, if you want more challenging work or if you feel that you have the ability to successfully change careers.

Don't be surprised if, at first, the thought of changing careers seems a little frightening. Most people are afraid, at least initially, to move from one field into another because it involves making changes that affect financial security. Generally, when women pursue a new career, they must endure a brief period of limited income until they are compensated by the new job.

In a culture that measures people by the amount of money they earn, most of us find that we shortchange ourselves by settling for material success only. Money is neither an essential qualification for achievement, nor is it an indication of success. Some individuals who have achieved great financial status have, in fact, achieved little else. Sometimes, in order to do what we love to do for a living and to become more worthwhile to ourselves in the process, it is necessary to scale down our lifestyles. Everyone, at some point in life, is faced with certain questions, such as, "What is it that makes me truly happy?" Or, "What possessions can I do without to obtain that happiness?" In the introduction to her book, *Do What You Love, The Money Will Follow*, Marsha Sinetar writes, "The task is easier than people imagine. All it takes is everything they have to give: all their talent, energy, focus, commitment and all their love. The rewards are worth it and are evident the minute one consciously chooses {a career option} on behalf of his or her own values, inclinations and vision."

Career Development

In today's world of work, more than at any other time in history, women are being offered more options for career choices. There are virtually hundreds of different career paths to take. Even if you are not yet sure about what you want to do with your career, you can take some action towards your professional future. The first step is to analyze your own values, interests and skills. If you find it difficult to make these evaluations independently, you can engage the help of a competent expert, such as a career counselor or a recruiter. Job counselors usually charge between $75 and $200 per session. The best way to locate a reputable counselor is through friends, colleagues or former business associates. You can also obtain the names of career counselors through local outplacement firms, career-development offices, psychologists, psychiatrists or your local chapter of the American Society for Training and Development.

Career-development sessions generally start off with a counselor giving you a series of written tests to determine your personal traits, interests, skills, aptitudes, value systems and career needs. Local universities and community colleges also offer individual or group career-counseling services free of charge or for a small fee. The book, *Full Potential*, by Robert J. Radin, Ph.D. (McGraw-Hill Co., New York, 1983) is another excellent career-planning guide. The exercises in this workbook will help you to probe your skills, values, or goals and to pinpoint what kind of work will best utilize your talents and satisfy your inner needs. *Full Potential* is for everyone, from the recent graduate to someone who has worked for years. It can be used to take the first important step: to change the course of a career that has already begun, or to switch careers altogether. The 1993 *What Color is Your Parachute?* by Richard Nelson Bolles (Ten Speed Press) is another practical manual for job-hunters and career changers. This up-to-date, 421-page guide has been redone nearly every year since 1970.

Once you have discovered your talents and have identified your skills, you can define specific career possibilities and research the type of job situation and working conditions that you think would be ideal. The best way to learn more about a field that interests you is to interview the people who are already doing well in it. Local resource centers can supply you with directories, job listings and files on specific fields, companies and employers. You can also contact your local library for more information.

To learn even more about the culture of the new field in which you are interested, and to acquire more information about the education and the skills you will need, volunteer your services to do small tasks after work or on weekends. The actual experience of working within your new field of interest will provide you with some insight into what it would be like to do that type of work and to determine if you are suited for it.

Once you have become acquainted with the work that you think you might like to do, and if you are still serious about changing your career, you will probably be faced with the challenge of retraining. If you have to return to school, you may be able to keep the job you have by taking a few classes part-time or in the evening.

Job Hunting

One of the best ways to find and to fill a new position is through "networking." Do not underestimate how many people you know and how many contacts they have. Inform everyone, including friends, colleagues, and significant business contacts, however remotely acquainted, that you are available. Notify everyone you can think of that you are looking for a job. Do not put them on the spot by asking for a position. Instead, ask for their advice in aiding your search. Career counselors and corporate recruiters suggest that if you hear of a specific opening for a job, request a meeting and offer to bring your resume with you.

Prepare for your interview by doing some research. Learn as much as you can about the position that is being offered and about the background of the company or organization. Make sure that the company supports diversity, that there are no artificial barriers to advancement, and that women are not excluded from top-level positions for reasons unrelated to their ability.

Executive Search Firms

Executive search firms define jobs and seek out candidates who qualify for them. To locate an executive recruiter, contact the trade association for your industry and ask for names. Be prepared to communicate to the recruiter exactly how much you require monetarily (salary, commissions, annual bonuses and increased earnings) as well as such other perks as health coverage, travel benefits and a retirement package.

Relocating

If career prospects are slim in your area, then relocating may be the answer to a more promising job market. Before you consider moving, however, determine if there is a demand for your profession nationally. It can take anywhere from four to eight months to find a white-collar job. So, be sure that you exhaust your home market first.

Another factor that you must weigh if you are thinking of moving is how well your family will adjust to relocating. Statistics indicate that adolescents are more affected by the separation from peers than are younger children. Although your spouse may be willing to accompany you, he may have to remain behind until he has a firm job offer. Gilbert Tweed Associates in New York offers Spouse-Search to help the relocating spouse find a job in a new area.

The Female Entrepreneur

Webster's Dictionary defines "entrepreneur" as "one who manages, and assumes the risks of, a business or enterprise." People who go into business for themselves display common characteristics. They are more willing to take chances on their financial security because they have a higher tolerance for uncertainty than most people have. They tend to be more disciplined and more focused, almost to the point of obsession.

Entrepreneurs thrive on challenges. It is the "contest" that motivates them and the need for personal achievement. Entrepreneurial women believe in their own personal resources: enthusiasm, energy, intelligence, and experience.

In the '90s, more women than ever before are going into business for themselves. Twenty-eight per cent of all businesses are now owned by women and 11 million jobs are provided by these businesses, according to a recent study conducted by the National Foundation of Women-Owned Business. According to the U.S. House of Representatives Committee on Small Business (1988), women will own 50% of all U.S. businesses by the year 2000. A mad rush to begin your own business venture is not always the wisest choice. Running a business is a complex affair that not everyone is equipped to handle. There are problems one must confront when self-employed. You must be able to make a realistic appraisal of your skills. Even though there are no educational requirements for starting your own business, going into business may require more experience and background than you currently possess. To be successful, you must be willing to obtain extra knowledge and to devote long hours to learning all that you can about the business in which you are interested.

The Small Business Administration (SBA) recommends that anyone considering their own business should personally rate themselves on the following list of personal traits and attitudes. To do so, place a check mark beside the description of the trait that you think applies to your personality and character.

The figures show that nearly two out of every three new businesses fail within the first five years. For this very reason, you should first seek professional advice if you are considering starting up your own company. It is wise to pay attention to established entrepreneurs who have had extensive experience owning and operating private businesses. A seasoned entrepreneur, one who is running the same type of enterprise you are interested in, can advise you about the challenges and hurdles you may have to face. Their expert advice can be extremely valuable and may save you from making serious mistakes during the early stages of growth and development.

One of the major reasons that most small companies fail is because there is not enough money "up front"... in other words, start up capital. According to the market-research firm, Venture Economics, to start a home-based business would cost about eight thousand dollars. This amount would cover only office supplies and equipment, not rent or insurance. Financing for other legitimate business expenses, such as inventory, advertising, raw materials and processing would also be needed. Start-up capital should include a reserve fund to cover financial setbacks and to keep the business afloat at least until the profits start coming in. Businesses that require capital investment generally take a year or more before they show a profit.

If you have considered going into business for yourself, have a very solid financial plan. One of the best sources of financial information is the Small Business Administration (SBA). The SBA is the

Personal Rating Chart for Potential Entrepreneurs

Initiative

☐ Additional tasks sought; highly ingenious
☐ Resourceful; alert to opportunities
☐ Regular work performed without waiting for directions
☐ Routine worker awaiting directions

Attitude Toward Others

☐ Positive; friendly interest in people
☐ Pleasant, polite
☐ Sometimes difficult to work with
☐ Inclined to be quarrelsome or uncooperative

Leadership

☐ Forceful, inspiring confidence and loyalty
☐ Order giver
☐ Driver
☐ Weak

Responsibility

☐ Responsibility sought and welcomed
☐ Accepted without protest
☐ Unwilling to assume without protest
☐ Avoided whenever possible

Organizing Ability

☐ Highly capable of perceiving and arranging fundamentals in logical order
☐ Able organizer
☐ Fairly capable of organizing
☐ Poor organizer

Industry

☐ Industrious; capable of working hard for long hours
☐ Can work hard, but not for too long a period
☐ Fairly industrious
☐ Hard work avoided

Decision

☐ Quick and accurate
☐ Good and careful
☐ Quick, but often unsound
☐ Hesitant and fearful

Sincerity

☐ Courageous, square-shooter
☐ On the level
☐ Fairly sincere
☐ Inclined to lack sincerity

Perseverance

☐ Highly steadfast in purpose; not discouraged by obstacles
☐ Effort steadily maintained
☐ Average determination and persistence
☐ Little or no persistence

Physical Energy

☐ Highly energetic at all times
☐ Energetic most of time
☐ Fairly energetic
☐ Below average

The majority of your check marks should be near the top of each section. If you find that most of them are near the bottom, you are probably not the best candidate for self-employment.

leading government-supported source for consulting on small business. SBA provides a wide range of counseling services that can help you get your new business up-and-running. In addition, you can obtain books and pamphlets on every aspect of business management, rules and regulations. These include: zoning, licenses and permits, safety and sanitation regulations, naming the business, trade names, trademarks, insurance, record-keeping, taxes, trade credit, bank loans and buying, renting and leasing equipment. Check the white pages of your telephone book under U.S. Government listings for the address of your nearest SBA office or write to the Small Business Administration, Washington D.C. 20416.

The U.S. Department of Commerce also offers free publications which analyze various businesses. The department has field offices located in various cities throughout the country. Also, contact your local chamber of commerce by phone, mail or personal appointment for additional pointers and information.

Banks, colleges and universities also offer a wide range of business counseling services and programs that are generally free. Also consider contacting a business consultant, a specially trained expert that can offer accurate, straightforward information to small companies, as well as to large corporations. Fees for professional consulting services vary, ranging from $100 to $1,000 per day.

A little patience, a little planning and a little luck can turn your dream of establishing a profitable, long-standing enterprise into a reality.

CHAPTER 4

Being Single and Successful

he relationship between men and women has never been a simple one. In fact, because of all of the social changes, today's standards, rules, and assigned roles are more confusing than ever. Not only are we witnessing a transfer of power, but it also appears that each sex is taking on some of the attributes of the other. Men are trying to become more in touch with their feelings and are taking a less liberal attitude toward sex without love. Women, though still in favor of meaningful relationships and marriage, are trying to retain their single status and independence longer in order to pursue their careers and self-development.

As women gain prominence, many are starting to question and, in some instances, even reject the traditional love, marriage and motherhood roles. As these old standards disappear, the sexes struggle to create new roles to replace them, improvising along the way. The most common approach seems to be to decide for one's self what is best, particularly when it comes to the issue of physical intimacy.

Sex in the '90s

Women in the '90s have no set standards of behavior to guide them when it comes to managing their sexual drive. One thing, however, is quite certain, with the increasing threat of AIDS and other sexually transmitted diseases: sexual freedom is starting to extend beyond the boundaries of safety. The single men and women of today are faced with a very serious dilemma. They are confronted with examining their own convictions about their sexuality The must decide whether to be sexually adventurous or to rigidly control their sexual urges.

It has been said that birth control did more to emancipate women than the right to vote. The transference of birth control from the male to the female had an enormous effect on male-female relationships. Without the threat of pregnancy, woman discovered that they, too, could have the prerogative of determining when, how often, and with whom they would have sexual relations.

The "sexual revolution" of the 1960s brought women's sexuality out into the open. Women had begun to experiment with their sexual potential. Many discovered that sex without love or premarital sex was hardly a crime. In fact, many found it to be quite delightful! Women liked the idea of being able to physically connect with someone, without having to commit themselves to a long-term relationship. No longer ashamed or embarrassed, women began talking about sex openly. In her book, *The Unmarried Woman's Guide To Men, Sex And The Single Girl*, Helen Gurley Brown writes, "Sex is a powerful weapon for a single woman in getting what she wants in life, i.e., a husband or steady male companionship. Sex is a more important weapon to the single woman than a married woman who has other things going for her—like the law!"

Women's freedom to make their own choices regarding their sexuality caused new patterns in male-female intimate relationships to emerge. It did not take long before the excesses of the sexual revolution became clear. Sex frequently became separated from true love, affection and intimacy. "One-night stands" became a common part of the dating scene. The closeness, familiarity, and honesty of lovemaking was absent. Women soon became aware that exerting their newfound, hard-won freedom was not without cost. Many women learned to become more independent, to be more particular with whom they slept, and to make choices that were true to their personal values. Many discovered that reserving sex for long-term relationships made it more fulfilling and meaningful.

The days of casual and carefree sexual involvement for both women and men are over. In the '90s, promiscuity is out. Many women are refusing dates from men who they are extremely attracted to physically because there is a high potential for sex. Though the old-fashioned Victorian taboos about sex are gone and premarital sex is no longer considered "morally wrong" socially, there is now a new set of restrictions being placed on female sexuality. Caution and fear are a part of every new sexual relationship. In addition to taking precautions to avoid unwanted pregnancies, women must take a strong stand on the importance of "safe sex." Single women must decide what course of action they will take to protect themselves against sexually transmitted diseases. Some women, terrified of being exposed to AIDS, insist on frank discussions before intimacy begins and on obtaining blood tests from potential partners. Still others are making a conscious decision to abstain from sex altogether.

Safe Sex

Women are constantly being bombarded with messages warning them to practice "safe sex." But, for some women, that is easier said than done. No woman in the early stages of romance likes to face the dread of questioning a potential lover about his past sexual relations. This often complicates the very vulnerable and still tentative relationship. Yet, women in this decade are being forced to do just that. They must not only equip themselves with condoms, but they must initiate intimate discussions with every new sexual partner on their use.

Women must address their own health needs while still facing the pressure of trying to please their sexual counterparts. Too many women, too often, are still left with persuading, begging, demanding, and employing every high and low pressure sales technique they can muster. All of this just to get the new man they are sleeping with to use a condom before becoming sexually intimate. Women who are engaging in unprotected sex, and believe that they could never contract the AIDS virus, are in denial and could end up paying with their lives. Just as women in the sexual revolution affirmed their right to sexual pleasure, in the '90s they must speak out for the right to be protected against AIDS and other deadly, sex-ually-transmitted diseases.

One very sure way to know if you or your partner is infected with the AIDS virus is to get tested. Women and their sexual part-ners who test "negative" for HIV (human immuno-deficiency virus, a virus that damages the human immune system) must wait three to four months and have absolutely no sexual exposure to HIV in the meantime. If they test negative again, only then can they be assured that they do not have the AIDS virus.

About Condoms

Condoms are the only form of birth control that also prevents the transmission of sexually transmitted diseases and AIDS. According to a 1993 study by the Centers for Disease Control (CDC), the proper and consistent use of latex condoms when engaging in sexual intercourse—vaginal, anal, or oral—can greatly reduce a per-son's risk of acquiring or transmitting sexually transmitted diseases (STDs), including HIV infection. If used properly, latex condoms are 98–100% effective, according to clinical studies by Italian researchers Saracco and Devincenzi. Condoms can be purchased at pharmacies and convenience, grocery, or health food stores.

There are two different types of condoms on the market: those constructed from natural membranes taken from the pouch-shaped part of the large intestine of a lamb; and latex condoms, made from a material that is derived from rubber trees. Although natural-mem-brane condoms are strong and feel more natural, they do not offer as much protection from sexually transmitted diseases as do con-doms made from latex. This is because natural membrane condoms are porous. Even though the pores are smaller than sperm in size, the pores of natural membrane condoms are ten times larger than the HIV virus that can lead to AIDS, and up to twenty-five times larger than the hepatitis-B virus.

A condom is only as strong as the thickness of the material that it is made of. Though thickness inhibits sensation for a man, thinner condoms may not offer as much protection because they can tear more easily. Condoms with a reservoir at the end (to collect semen), are safer because this additional space prevents breakage. If you are going to use a condom with a spermicide (a jelly that attacks sperm and certain forms of bacteria that kill sexually transmitted diseases), be sure to check the expiration date. If they are stored properly, they can last from two to five years.

Condoms made from latex need to be protected from artificial light, sunlight and heat. They should not be kept in pockets or wallets. Instead, they should be stored in a cool, dry area to protect the latex from drying out. Before using a condom be sure to check it for holes or tears. If the condom feels sticky, it is defective and must be replaced.

To apply the condom properly, unroll it over the entire penis. To prevent breakage, make sure the vagina is sufficiently lubricated. A soluble lubricant, like K-Y jelly, contraceptive jelly, cream or foam can be used. Never use baby oil or petroleum jelly with latex condoms because the oil will weaken the material. After ejaculation, the condom should be removed before the penis becomes soft. To avoid spillage, the condom should be held close to the base of the penis. The penis should not touch any part of the vagina once the condom is removed because it may still have live sperm on it.

Celibacy

The urge to have sexual relations is a basic desire of human existence. As a culture, we have been trained to believe that to reject sex would be to repress our own natural instincts. We live in a society that says that if we can not fulfill our primitive desires, we are seriously jeopardizing our well-being.

There used to be a popular notion that if a bachelorette abstained from sex it was because she had a history of deeply rooted sexual inhibition. In other words, she must have been using celibacy as a means to camouflage her frigidity. In the past, this pervasive form of cultural conditioning played an important role in how celibacy had been viewed. But, this is no longer the case because of the alarming rise of sexually transmitted diseases, especially AIDS. Today, celibacy has gained new popularity. In fact, a growing number of single women believe that the advantages of celibacy far outweigh the disadvantages. More than a few single women believe that sex seems like more trouble than it's worth. These women are anything but prudish; they just feel that there are not a lot of males out there who are worth jeopardizing their health for.

Not all single women have to be involved in a sexual relationship or preoccupied with the emotional status of one. Tired of shallow encounters with men, some women go for months and even years without having sexual relations. They claim that these periods of abstinence provide them with an opportunity to learn more about themselves. Another great benefit of practicing abstinence is that it provides women with time to examine their relationships with men and to determine who and what they really want in a relationship.

Suddenly Single

In this decade, separation from a loved one, either voluntarily or through divorce or death, is part of our social reality. Disappointed with unsatisfactory relationships and in touch with their own potential, more and more women are choosing to abandon long-term affairs and loveless marriages. Up until recently, only a courageous few had seized the opportunity to leave their heartbreak and troubled lives behind them in order to return to a single life in search of healthier relationships. There are a growing number of women who think differently now, mainly because of their socio-economic strength and personal competence. More independent than ever, they see themselves as being successful in their own right.

Involuntarily Single

Not all women wish nor do they choose to be liberated from the traditional female roles as wife, mother and homemaker. For such women, the single life holds no appeal. They are not intentionally unattached. They would prefer to be involved in a loving partnership. However, for one reason or another, they have not been able to secure nor to commit to a serious, long-term relationship.

It is difficult to function as a single woman in a society that presents marriage to young women as a natural transition into womanhood. Some single women become frantic in their desire to find someone to whom they can be connected, and in the process, lose all sense of self. They so desperately yearn for wholeness that they substitute the type of companion they really want for a man they can easily get. Women who buy into the belief that "a woman's proper place is in a traditional marriage," and marry merely to fulfill that role, will probably end up in a failed marriage. Women need to get past their false desires for marriage and really question their fantasies. By accepting the truth about what they really need in a lasting union, they can resist the temptation to surrender to the first man who pops the question.

The Never-Ending Quest For Mr. Right

Although some women have great personal expectations, ambitions and drive, they believe that they must find just the right man before they can feel complete. They are caught in a trap of forever hoping that they will someday meet the perfect partner. These "searcher women" set incredibly high standards for their male prospects to live up to. They are often skeptical and cynical about the men they meet or become involved with. Their strict criteria protects their single status so that they can continue to enjoy the freedom of self-indulgence, which includes living alone, traveling, and discretionary spending habits. All the while they appear as if they are succumbing to the social pressure to marry. Single yet hopeful, they feel they can have the best of both worlds: the protection of "singlehood" and the constant thrill of pursuing the ideal mate.

Divorced With Children

Divorced women with children must deal with more than merely patching up their stormy lives; they have the equally urgent task of single-parenting before them. Their newfound freedom is overshadowed by larger issues that they must confront immediately such as the uncertainty of their children's future.

Every mother who loves her children has known the experience of not being able to meet all of their needs either because of financial restrictions or from emotional or physical exhaustion. But, try to imagine the demands of motherhood without the critical contribution of child support from the co-parent. Many fathers deny their financial responsibility and refuse to pay child support. Very few divorced women with children are financially in a position to be the head of the household.

Even when the ex-husband does pay child support, it is never enough to offset the cost of raising children. It is not uncommon for a single mother to work more than one job just to make ends meet. In her book The Dollars and Sense of Divorce, Judith Briles writes, "Getting a job is not the only answer. It is not a guaranteed way out of poverty. In fact, one-third of the divorced women cannot earn enough to enable them to live above the poverty level." Living "hand-to-mouth" is a despairing situation which many single mothers are finding themselves in nowadays.

Because of long work hours and time spent with children, freedom for dating is limited. Financial restrictions further diminish recreation and leisure activities. Night clubs and dances somehow lose their glamour to a woman who has to constantly compromise and make concessions for her children.

Divorced women with children must work twice as hard during their period of readjustment. Repairing, resolving, and healing the wounds of the past are needed so that their hurts are not inherited by their offspring. Children can be reminders of painful, failed relationships. The single, divorced mother must take on the responsibility of re-inventing her own life. Furthermore, she is faced with the enormous task of rebuilding the lives of her children as well.

Children require intensive care and intimacy. Raising children by oneself is time-consuming and expensive. There are no shortcuts when it comes to single-parenting. A single mother will generally look out for her children's needs first. She is likely to dismiss romance and look, instead, for a companion who is hard-working, reliable, a good provider, and who will form an attachment to her children.

Single mothers must be careful not to use their children as an excuse for denying their own needs for affection, love and intimacy. If they do not take responsibility for fulfilling some of their own requirements their children could easily become objects of their repressed anger and frustration.

Regardless of what issues a woman may be facing, one thing is certain: reentry into the single's world is not easy. When we leave a dysfunctional relationship, we often feel worse before we feel better. But with a little clever maneuvering, women can flourish as well as survive.

Affairs With Married Men

The number of relationships between married men and single women have greatly increased over the past decade and they appear to be on the rise. Though many of the women engaged in these extramarital affairs will be married, the greater number of such women will be single.

It would be futile to attempt to stereotype all of the various single women who are presently involved with married men. Some can be considered plain-looking, while others are attractive, even beautiful. Some are fashionable; some unkempt. Others are unskilled and some are competent professionals. The most common misconception of "the mistress" is that of a single woman who is financially cared for by her married lover. This may have been true in the past. Today, however, many women who are involved with married men support themselves.

The reasons why women become involved in extramarital affairs vary. Single women who are afraid of committing to a serious relationship will often end up having an affair with a married man. Married lovers are especially appealing to single, career-orientated women because they are less demanding than a spouse or a live-in boyfriend. Single and content, these women are too active in their careers to assume the responsibilities of married life. They may eventually want to settle down, but not until their earnings, experience, maturity and attitude are such that they feel ready. A single women may also see a married man as an answer to her financial or sexual problems.

Not all single women who become entangled in extramarital affairs do so knowingly. Some men enjoy being married but like to pretend they are single when the opportunities prevail. Such men may lie and say that they are separated or in the process of getting a divorce. By the time the single woman figures out that her new lover already has a wife and children (and tries to break off the relationship), it is often too late. She is already emotionally attached.

It is very easy for "the other woman" to become emotionally dependent upon her married lover. She becomes accustomed to him setting the rules as to when they can be together. He arranges all of their meetings. He comes and goes at the drop of a hat, often drifting in and out of her life with very little notice. Some single women end up planning their entire schedules around their married boyfriends. They become hopelessly addicted to the few treasured moments that they spend together.

An affair with a married man can last for months, years, or even decades. Eventually, however, it will end. When the breakup does come, it almost always seems as if the married man has won. He may end the relationship because of a career promotion that forces him to move away. Another reason may be because his wife has presented him with an ultimatum. Finally, there is always the probability that his lover may be replaced by a new girlfriend.

Circumstances may influence men to cheat on their wives, but few will actually leave them. Statistics show that if a man who is having an extramarital affair does divorce, he will not necessarily end up marrying his concubine. Although the single woman plays an important part in her married lover's life, when a man "cuts the cord" he usually discards everything and everyone connected with the memory of his marriage.

When the single woman can no longer stand it, the affair ends. The longer the affair lasts, the harder and the more painful it is for "the other woman" to withdraw. The trauma from the separation can produce intense emotional reactions. There is a continued feeling of attachment, even though she may want to put the affair behind her; but the links to the past remain. As the initial shock of the breakup subsides, the tendency is to remember the happy times. To terminate the relationship, "the other woman" may have to go through a series of false endings. The temptation to work things out and to slip back into the relationship is very strong. The single woman's resolve is further weakened by periods of yearning to be with her married lover. There is the feeling that everything will be all right if only they could be together again.

The emotional aftermath of the terminated affair can be devastating. A common response is that of guilt and self- blame, most of it for being naive and overly trusting. "The other woman" lives a fantasy life up until the affair ends. Once reality sets in, she discovers that the dashing man whom she loves is merely fiction. Married men do lie, cheat and make false promises.

Because of the secrecy surrounding an affair, "the other woman" is often reluctant to discuss the intimate details of her relationship. As a result, she has very little support, if any, from her family or from her inner circle of friends when the relationship ends. Although we live in a rapidly changing society, we are still a long way from accepting extra-marital affairs. A mistress cannot command the same respect and sympathy that a divorced woman or widow can. As a rule, the few friends she does confide in are unsympathetic because the man she was involved with was married. She often finds herself alone and with no one to really talk to concerning her feelings. Abandoned by her lover, whatever agony and disgrace she experiences will all belong to her alone.

In the long run, an extramarital affair just doesn't pay off. In fact, being "the other woman" can have serious psychological consequences. The loss of a married lover on whom a woman has lavished her entire love, and on whom she has depended so completely for financial sustenance and moral support, is bound to have a profound effect on her. She has had to forfeit her happiness as payment for her mistake of falling in love with a man who is unfaithful to his wife. The overwhelming despair from the breakup can last for months or even years. It can cost the single woman her financial security and self-respect, not to speak of the mental anguish involved. Worst of all, she is at risk of losing something of much greater value: her sense of identity.

Having an affair with a married man doesn't necessarily equal unhappiness. In all fairness, one could, of course, quote cases of extramarital affairs that have had positive endings. It would be presumptuous to say that every woman who is involved with a married lover is insecure and seeks out destructive relationships. Some single women are willing to gamble and to face the consequences of being involved in an extramarital affair. Aware of the risk they are taking, they are able to keep their emotions in check. They often feel they can avoid making mistakes that may seriously hurt them. They are not bothered by the opinions of others; they become immune to criticism or close scrutiny. As women become more like men in their view of the world, so, too, can they adopt the casual attitude of some married men about extra-marital affairs.

Going For The Gold

Some women are looking for a man with a substantial will, one that is eventually be the beneficiary of. If it is riches you seek, just remember: the woman who dates or marries for money usually earns every penny of it.

Almost all women have fantasies about being in a relationship with a wealthy man. However, most men of fortune are extremely ambitious. During the initial stages of a relationship, such men can be very attentive, but as the relationship progresses, it is usually their love for money that controls their hearts. Men who lose themselves in their work tend to neglect their wives and children. Life can be unbearably lonely for a woman involved in such an alliance. Material things make terrible substitutes for real love, companionship and joy.

Another drawback of marrying strictly for care and protection is that the women who marry for money must continually fight to attract and to keep their provider's attention. To ensure their lavish lifestyle, they must remain appealing. Instead of helping their mate produce income, their job is to create a wonderful home life and support their husbands drive for status. If the marriage does not work out, and their husband tires of them, they divorce them, and marry more capable and independent women that they admire. Divorce has proven to be a difficult transition stage for these women. Suddenly, the full-time wife with no work experience outside the home is told to get out and get a job. And, after all her years of dedication, the homemaker cannot even file for unemployment benefits.

Younger Men and Older Women

In the past, it was rare to see an older woman involved with a younger man. Recently, however, such relationships are emerging as a recognizable social pattern for intelligent, accomplished, middle-aged women. This is because men who are the most educated and most occupationally situated tend to settle down early. This leaves a number of women who are over the age of 25 without potential marriage partners. Men in their forties and beyond characteristically marry women who are ten years younger than themselves. What this tells us is that single women, after a certain age, have less of the male population to choose from.

In an effort to compensate for the shortage of eligible males, some women will ultimately choose to overlook the age factor. They will seek romantic fulfillment through intimate relationships with younger men.

For women, becoming involved with men much younger than themselves means facing and overcoming the fear of social rejection. Through the years, women have been belittled by our society for taking the romantic initiative with men. Customarily, they are taught to remain passive until the man to whom they are attracted makes the first move. Women are expected to wait for the follow-up phone call and the sexual request. In contrast, a woman who seeks a younger lover is more assertive.

As women become more successful and more financially independent in their own right, they have more freedom to indulge in
their romantic fantasies. Men have always selected women to whom
they are physically attracted and women certainly have a right to a
similar physical preference. In fact, it appears that quite a few mature
women find younger men more to their liking. According to the
National Center of Health Statistics, almost one-quarter of the marriages that took place in 1988 were between older women and
younger men.

More often than not, an accomplished middle-aged woman
will single out a younger man because he is in his prime; she expects
sex with him will be terrific. Research indicates that women become
more orgasmic when they reach their thirties because their bodies
produce more testosterone (the male hormone responsible for sex
drive). Men, however, reach their sexual peak around their late teens
and early twenties. As men approach their middle years, they have
less energy and their interest in sex decreases. At ages 45 or 50, it
takes longer for a man to achieve an erection; it takes only seconds
in youth. Most men at mid-life do not make love as often as younger
men and do not always respond adequately to their partner's interest. Sexually, a man who is five to fifteen years younger than a
woman, often provides what many older men can not: a serviceable
physical relationship. Sex is bound to be good when it is exciting and
more frequent.

Good sex is not the only reason women are drawn to men
who are younger than themselves. Another factor that makes young
adult males so appealing is that they have fewer macho and chau-
vinistic tendencies than mature men. Younger men appear to be
more sensitive and caring than most older men are. They tend to be
open and more willing to communicate their feelings. Women credit
their young partners with being more flexible in adapting to events
and transitions.

Naturally, dating or marrying a younger man can have its drawbacks. When a mature woman is to be seen with her young lover in public, it is with the knowledge that unwanted female attention will be part of the package. In some instances, this can be a very humbling experience. On occasion, a young mate can be perceived by onlookers as a son. Initially, such a dilemma can bring on a sense of frustration and embarrassment. However, the indiscretions of others, if handled appropriately, can be an inside joke for the two lovers to share.

A liaison with a younger man can certainly have its unpleasant aspects. This is especially true if a young man has a hidden agenda and is really looking for a surrogate mother, mentor, or teacher. Unfortunately, the mothering that most young men receive in a romantic relationship of this sort (with a woman who is seeking to recapture the powers of her own youth), is not enough. Such a male partner needs constant approval and requires a great deal of attention. A relationship of this sort is headed for disaster because it lacks the rich, rewarding experiences of genuine sharing. It works only as long as the mature woman can justify the emotional drain of a partner who is wholly dependent upon her and she doesn't feel as if she is being taken advantage of.

Not every woman is willing to take the risk of becoming involved with a younger man. Some women may fear that their young lovers will lose interest in them as their older female lover visibly ages faster than their companion. The threat of abandonment diminishes, however, when women discover that they can take care of themselves. After all, any relationship is a gamble and can break up at any time. One last positive note: according to statistics, most women are widowed at age sixty-five; you will not be one of them if you marry a man fifteen to twenty years younger.

How to Successfully Cope With A Failed Relationship

Rejection and failed relationships are inevitable in the mating game. When a woman is rejected or her relationship fails, she is often left emotionally vulnerable and confused. The following emotions are commonly associated with a failed relationship: embitterment, rage, disillusionment, feelings of isolation and loneliness, depression and shattered self-esteem.

Following is a list of ten suggestions that will help put you back on track so that you can weather the sorrows of rejection.

---

10 Suggestions for Coping With a Failed Relationship

1. The first step of the healing process is to experience the emotional pain that accompanies your loss. Give yourself permission to be absolutely brokenhearted.

2. Call your friends and ask for their support. Cry it out if you need to.

3. Take some time off from work, if necessary, to recover from your emotional wounds. However, be sure to put a time limit on your grieving period.

4. Document your feelings about the breakup in a journal. Write out a list of everything about this person that you never liked. Be sure to record every time he had disappointed you by breaking dates or by not calling. Look over what you have written and try to make a realistic assessment of your relationship.

5. Scrutinize your behavior. Ask yourself if your involvement with this man was a healthy one. Go back farther and compare this relationship to your last one to determine if there are any similarities. Search for a pattern. Be your own judge. Use the breakup as an opportunity to gain some understanding from your mistakes.

6. Eliminate all contact with your "ex." Do not call him or accept calls or letters from him.

7. Sever ties with any mutual friends the two of you may have had. Then, when you regain your emotional strength, you can separate them from your "ex." Be prepared, though, because some of the friends you've shared are likely to become his allies, confidants, and rescuers. Ultimately, you will lose if you try to force them into taking your side.

7. Avoid places where the two of you may have gone together.

8. Consider refurbishing your wardrobe, re-styling or coloring your hair.

9. Circulate socially; do not isolate yourself. Accept invitations. Give yourself a chance to meet new people and make new friends.

10. Get involved in a new activity that will enhance your self-esteem. Take up a foreign language. Learn photography. Attend cooking classes or adult fitness courses. Learn to speed read or take a drama class. Whether you realize it or not you are "playing a part" everyday. Are you playing your role with authority and self-confidence? Learn to play the part of the person you really want to be.

———————————

Be patient. With the passage of time, you will discover that you can cope. Eventually, you will make a complete recovery. Once you have started to adjust to the loss of your ex, you can set about finding his replacement. Let it be someone who will recognize and appreciate you for all of the wonderful things that you are.

Attracting Men

Though a professional woman may want a career, she will probably have no objection to a love interest or to marriage. Just because a woman is top-notch in her field, it does not automatically insure that she will have the same success in her personal life. Men don't necessarily view an educated, accomplished, professional woman as superior to other women. Some men, in fact, are really turned off by high status, career oriented women. Unlike women who were brought up to marry men of power, men have a different set of standards for selecting a mate. Men claim to be infatuated with women who are physically attractive, who have a good sense of humor, and who are warm, loving and, most of all, emotionally stable. Even though they enjoy the company of an intelligent female, they don't seem to believe that this is the most important factor in choosing a companion.

Sadly, too many single women undervalue themselves. The way in which a man responds to a woman generally depends upon how the woman treats herself and what she believes she deserves. No one else will give us value until we first give value to ourselves. Make a careful study of yourself. Correct your flaws, if possible, and accept your imperfections. Enhance the good points of your personality so that you can present a positive view to the world. A woman who is self-assured and confident is extremely attractive to men.

Where To Make Romantic Contacts

Fifty years ago, single women were expected to meet men exclusively through their families and close friends, or through work, school and social gatherings. Today, we live in a different world. More single women than ever before are breaking the bonds of established social behavior; they are taking the initiative by seeking out the men who interest them.

The easiest way to meet new men is to be alert to chance encounters. The world is filled with men. Look at the happenings of your daily life. Most single women are surrounded by interesting men all day long, but their dedication to a formalized routine isolates them. They become too preoccupied with their business and with hurrying around. Become more aware of your habits and behavior. You can inadvertently alienate men by being inattentive. Take time out to carefully observe the men around you. Acquire a new philosophy. One of the major stumbling blocks in the path of women seeking to meet new men is their own attitude. When you have begun to notice men more as people rather than as potential partners, you will find them to have some very engaging qualities. Often, they are worth getting to know.

The following list will provide you with just a few of the many places where single women can come into contact with eligible men:

Health clubs	Airports
Professional conferences	Department stores
Parties	(in the men's dept.)
Art galleries	Supermarkets
Museums	Cultural affairs
Bookstores	Public libraries
Lectures	Local clubs
Political rallies	Fund-raising events
Sporting events	Tennis courts
Recreation centers	Delicatessens
Restaurants	Bakeries
Golf courses	Apartment complexes

Making Initial Contact

If you find yourself in a situation with a man to whom you are strongly attracted, send out social signals that indicate you are approachable. Demonstrate your willingness for contact through your body language. Make eye contact, smile, move closer to him and position yourself in his line of vision. Try to establish a rapport by engaging him in a conversation that will result in a response from him. Open the conversation with comments on the moment. For example, make a casual observation about something in your immediate environment; ask him a question or compliment him on his clothing or grooming. When speaking to him, convey warmth and sincerity in your voice. If, after meeting him you surmise that he doesn't interest you very much (not all casual contacts will result in rewarding involvement), remember that you are in no way committed to dating him.

Living Single and Liking It

According to "A Second Chance at Love," an article in *Redbook Magazine*, April 1992, "Adults who never marry—both men and women—are an expanding segment of the population. In 1988, 8.7% of adults over 35 had never been married, as opposed to 6% in 1980. This trend may reflect changing social attitudes about the need for marriage." Today, numerous women are living single and enjoying it. They no longer feel that they need to cling to a man for economic security. There isn't the need to parade him around as a trophy in order to feel important. Single women do not expect a man to give them an identity or to be life's antidote. They are relying solely upon themselves, managing to meet their own needs and enjoying true personal independence.

There are definite advantages to being single. There are incredible feelings of personal strength, serenity in the home, privacy, the freedom to travel or to go wherever your spirit takes you and, most importantly, the opportunity to expand social relations and special interests. Whatever her choices, the single woman makes them, they are hers, and she has the freedom to live with them.

Career and Marriage

*T*he professional woman has definite responsibilities to both her family and her job. Juggling a career and a personal life is not easy. Difficult though the career and marriage combination may be, there is a way to cope with the responsibilities of full-time employment, a husband and children. Today women can have it all but only if they give it their all. This chapter focuses on dual-career issues and addresses the delicate balance between marriage, motherhood and career.

Meet Debbie, an attractive, highly educated woman in her mid-thirties. Debbie is the mother of two small children; she is also an attorney. In fact, she graduated from one of the top law schools in the nation. She makes a large salary and is married to a man who makes an even larger salary. To the casual observer she appears composed. She makes being a breadwinner, homemaker and mother look effortless. But behind the mask of self-assurance hides a woman in crisis. She is at her wits' end. She is all tangled up in the complexities of managing both a career and a family life. She is torn between her vocational commitment and the guilt that accompanies being a working wife and mother. She could probably maintain the pretense indefinitely if it were not for the crying spells, insomnia, depression, and her inability to concentrate. She disguises her exhaustion, conceals her frustration and lives with her guilt. No matter how others may view her, she feels inadequate inside. She is "playing a part."

Women in the '90s are challenged with playing a multitude of roles: part-time wife, part-time mother, career woman, and others. Those of us who have tried know that the demands associated with maintaining the home and nurturing the family often conflict with the responsibilities associated with a professional career. In a working culture that has double standards for women, it is not uncommon for a female professional to be called away from the office so she can go home to care for her sick child. Yet, rarely does one hear of a professional man leaving work to deal with family health problems.

Worn to a frazzle by the frantic pace that must be kept to meet the demands of job and family, many women feel chronically rushed. Trapped in an unrelenting time crunch, they are constantly shuffling, rescheduling, shifting or rearranging. They are overwrought, over-committed and under-valued. Women who work outside the home are beginning to realize that they must devise an array of "coping strategies" to make all the pieces of the puzzle fit.

With a double income, a married couple could once have afforded many of the things that might otherwise haven take them years to acquire. But, in recent times, more and more women are coming to the realization that holding down a job is more of a necessity than an option. In the '90s, married women are expected to contribute to the financial needs of their households. Without their salary, especially in today's economy, it would be impossible for their family to maintain a decent standard of living. Not only does the working wife's extra income provide a significant subsidy, but in many instances it provides her family with additional benefits such as health care.

Fortunately, most women choose to work. Having a job makes them feel productive, independent, and better about themselves. Many working mothers claim that their hectic schedule becomes overwhelming only when they are unable to spend enough time with their children. In short, Debbie's experience as a working wife and mother is no longer the exception. The most important thing to Debbie is that she doesn't have to choose between her career and her children. In an era where her grueling routine is not extraordinary, she considers herself lucky to have both a stimulating job and a rich family life. She knows that most women experience some guilt con-nected with being a working wife and parent. However, by juggling both roles, Debbie feels she is setting an example for her daughter. She is showing her that it is not easy. But then she says, "Life is not easy." At least today it is possible for a woman "to have it all."

Working women can successfully fill occupational and marital roles simultaneously but there is always going to be some loss. This is our predicament. Every time we progress in the direction of our loved ones or in the direction of our career, we disconnect the two roles. At least for that period of time, we forfeit one for the other. Each role has it pitfalls and it's advantages. Choices must be made and a constant attempt to constitute a crucial balance is imperative. We must not lose hope; there are workable solutions.

Other important changes need to be made. First, the business world must acknowledge and respect the female professional's commitment to her family. As a nation we need to devise a way for one parent to be home with a new baby during its first year of life in order to prevent maternal deprivation. Job flexibility needs to be offered to working mothers, with more flextime and part-time options to accommodate family responsibilities. Childcare programs need to be developed to provide on-site, high-quality day care centers. This would reduce the amount of time during which working mothers would be separated from their children.

Working women need to ask for, and need to receive, more help from their spouses. They need husbands who will support their work in the home by sharing equal responsibility for domestic chores and child-rearing.

Professional career women should also allow themselves the option of receiving outside assistance to help meet household responsibilities. There are many competent caregivers who can be brought into the home on a permanent or part-time basis to relieve the strain of carrying a full load of housework and caring for children.

Career Fulfillment

To be really happy in her career a woman must do something she truly loves. It is a tremendous pleasure and a real thrill to derive a living from stimulating work. Being excited about what one does makes it easier to work extra hard. Additional effort is always required for achievement. When a woman is interested in what she does she is apt to learn more and progress faster in her career.

Sometimes, in the search for balance in life, a woman discovers that she needs to consider making a career change. This is especially true if the job she has is not helping her to achieve self-fulfillment. When a job becomes more static than dynamic, it is time to make a change. We spend more of our waking hours at work than anywhere else. This is why it is vital to our physical and mental health that we look forward to going to work everyday.

Tapping into our natural attributes is the best way to discover our earning power. To determine our full potential we must be able to identify our talents and our skills. Women need to celebrate their personalities and their inborn traits that make them unique. By organizing our individual strengths we can locate and create the greatest career opportunities for ourselves.

If a woman is at a job that she is not happy with but cannot leave, then she should find something about her work upon which she can improve. The fastest way to mend a negative outlook is to explore what facets of our work we do enjoy and then to expand on them.

Women And Finances

In our culture, men are considered the chief workers and have long been thought of as the primary breadwinners outside of the home environment. We can see how men's roles are changing and how the husband-father no longer possess all the authority. But many men still think of themselves as head of the family. Such men feel that they represent their wives and children outside the home and that their chief obligation is to protect their loved ones. Even today, both social and religious customs give credence to this concept of male dominion despite the fact that the structure of the family is in a major transitional stage.

Since women have joined the workforce, National Center of Health studies show, half of all the marriages in this country end in divorce. One of the reasons may be because the traditional role of the husband as "head of the household" has changed and along with it so have the responsibilities and privileges that went with the title. Gone are the days when a husband could borrow, buy or sell and commit his wife in financial matters without her knowledge or approval. In sharp contrast, today, because so many women are dual-wage earners, women not only expect to have a definite say in money matters but are starting to insist that their husbands view them as equal partners in all financial transactions. Married couples argue more about how to spend their money than over their money problems.

Friction between marriage partners occurs when one spouse has a different view on how their money should be spent. Traditionally, housewives were given an allowance and assigned to do all the buying for the household. The larger purchases were discussed and the husband acted as the purchasing agent for the entire family. Until recently, before so many wives became part of the work force, husbands had the ultimate authority in financial decisions.

More and more women are now taking an active part in financial planning, money management, and in determining their economic future. No longer relying on their husbands to make all their financial decisions for them, married women who work and contribute their paychecks to the support of the household have more of a voice in family financial matters. They have more control over spending than their grandmothers or their mothers did. They know how much it costs them to live, where their money is being spent, and in many cases how they want to invest it.

Unfortunately, some women who are "earning their keep" are still battling for equal participation in financial decisions. For them arguing with their husbands about spending may be more of a power struggle than a fight over money. Wives who are married to husbands with old-fashioned, fixed ideas about money are growing increasingly more antagonistic. However, despite how tough the struggle is to win equality, most women claim they still prefer to battle it out. Women have learned, through past experience, that there is a much higher cost associated with financial dependence.

In all fairness to men, they are not the only ones who have old-fashioned ideas about money. Some women consider their husband's salary as joint income, but their salary as theirs alone. They refuse to contribute their fair share to help relieve financial pressures. Instead they spend their money lavishly or indiscriminately and develop extravagant habits that produce debt. Such women also have outdated ideas about money. They still see their husbands in the role of provider or protector and their salary as nothing more than extra spending money or small change. Nothing is more destructive to the future security of a women than the false assumption that she will always be provided for by her husband. For every married woman regardless of her age, there looms the possibility of divorce or widowhood. All women need to take personal responsibility for their finances and join their husbands in planning out their financial future.

Career, Marriage, And Conflict

If a woman is very successful in her career and ends up earning more money than her husband, her success could cause a significant problem in her marriage—especially, if her husband does not view women as equal to men. He may feel threatened by his wife's professional achievements, particularly if his wife earns more money than he does.

Matthew's role in the family scenario was that of major provider. Matthew and his wife Carolyn were both computer programmers and had equal qualifications. Although his wife Carolyn was very successful in her own right and worked every bit as hard as her husband, she had not received the same monetary compensation. Having reached the glass ceiling in her position, she felt as if she was fighting a losing battle. As time went by, she became more and more disenchanted until finally she decided to leave the company and find another job. At first, Matthew was supportive of Carolyn's decision to try to advance her career until she landed a position that paid her more than Matthew. Deep down, Matthew feared total equality between Carolyn and him. Suddenly, Matthew begin to sabotage Carolyn's career. He complained loudly and abusively when she would inform him she had to work late. He would plan last minute vacations when he knew she would be out of town on business and then would become enraged when she would not cancel her business trips. He made her feel she was incompetent as a wife and mother by constantly ridiculing her in front of their children and their friends. He would humiliate her by discussing intimate details about their personal life at social gatherings. Invariably, Matthew's contentious attitude led to their divorce.

Many women so fear this sort of backlash that they jeopardize their own career. The fear of succeeding in the work world of men compels them to deliberately reject or sabotage career opportunities that might mean a greater difference in earnings or status from their husbands.

In some cases women even down-play career achievements to prevent their husbands from feeling inferior or inept. In 1968, a study was made in which 178 female undergraduates from the University of Michigan participated. The Horner study concluded that women feel that if they succeed in their career, then they are not living up to societal expectations about the female role. Passivity, dependency, and incompetence in the world outside the home were considered female qualities. Even today, according to Martha Friedman, in her book, *Overcoming The Fear Of Success*, "There are few woman at the top of their profession. There are too many societal and parental negative messages with which a woman executive must deal before she can effectively face the built-in problems of a woman in a man's business world."

Men with a weak sense of self will over-identify with their job status and how much they earn. To them, the recognition they get from their career achievements and the money they make is an indicator confirming their self-worth. This type of man is unsure of himself and is insecure to begin with, and therefore is more likely to feel threatened by his wife's success. A woman who makes more money than her husband should try to be more emotionally attentive to him, and offer him more affection, support and reinforcement. This is essential to balancing the relationship. Another way to solve the unequal income problem is for the wife to combine her earnings with those of her husband; this will reduce the discrepancy. A man and his wife need not be equals to each other, just fundamental parts of each other's reality.

Household Management

The romantic notion of home evokes a reverie of tender, enduring, happy memories that return again and again to capture the simple delights of our youth. For those of us fortunate enough to grow up in a stable living environment, the word *home* fills our minds with sudden nostalgia. It conjures up visions of childhood as we recall the simple pleasures associated with such an extraordinary place.

A home has all the subtleties that transform a vacant area into a cozy living space. In addition to where we cook, eat, sleep, and bathe, it is where we entertain our closest friends and raise our family. More of a concept than a look, it is a feeling that projects well beyond the walls of a mere shelter. To many, home is a symbol of family life and well-being.

The distinctive style of where we live reflects our individual taste and is an extension of our personality. We all have our own idealized version of what home is. To a working woman who lives in the suburbs, home may be a two-story house with a private yard for her children to play in or a quiet retreat many miles from the over-crowded, noisy world of the big city. To the city dweller, home may be an apartment in a high-rise structure at the center of a densely populated area or a towering edifice offering privacy and discouraging interaction between neighbors. But, whether we perceive the word *home* as a cottage or a sleek condo, as a place for quiet contemplation, or an area designated for carefree activity, a home should be a refuge that offers asylum from a fast-paced, hurry-up world.

As wonderful as it may be, the home of a working professional also has its dark side. Maintaining and running an active household is an endless task. No professional woman deserves to put in a full eight to ten hours at the office just to come home to a mess. Disarray leads to chaos, and chaos adds to stress.

In the past, social conditioning made women feel as if they should totally dedicate themselves to the care of their home and family. They took pride in homemaking, devoting themselves above all else to cleaning, rearing their children and entertaining. Even today, society expects that women be selfless, giving and all-capable. As a result, many working women feel that when it comes to their home life, they come up short. They feel that the pressures and stress of managing both family life and career is an inherent part of modern life. When the pressure's on, women tend to intensify their efforts to be the perfect wives, mothers and homemakers. They push themselves to the limits, and often beyond, to reassure themselves of their womanhood.

Statistics from the U.S. Department of Labor indicate that women constitute the largest work force in the country. The figures confirm that over 55% of women today work outside the home. A woman that holds down a full-time job simply does not have the time to cook, clean and care for her family as elaborately as her mother did. The working professional's time is limited. It is unrealistic, and even destructive, for women who are deeply involved in a career to try to maintain such outmoded beliefs. Although many women will not admit it, the truth is that they still hang on to remnants of those old-fashioned beliefs.

A Women's Home Should Be Her Castle

There is a special significance and sacredness attached to a wholesome home life. A woman who does her day's work deserves a clean, well-organized place where she can come home, lock the door behind her and feel safe. She needs a place where she can house her most cherished mementos and precious treasures. She needs a warm and cozy sanctuary where she can unwind, relax or re-energize. She needs a place where she can read by a window and sleep soundly through the night. The working woman's home should be a friendly dwelling that offers comfort and emulates peace and contentment. Regardless of whether she is married or single, whether her residence is a five-bedroom house in an outlying community or a one-room studio in the heart of the city, her home should be an inviting, welcoming place that offers relief from the pressures of the day.

If women are going to have a healthy balance between their professional and personal lives, then they are going to have to develop a balanced outlook. They will need to re-examine their core values and the things they cherish. They must take a closer look at the essentials in their life that contribute to their well-being, such as their home and their family. Then, they must integrate these elements with their way of living.

One of the greatest tragedies of our modern civilization is the speed at which we are living. With less free time, there is also less time for housework. At the hour when most people get off work, the day is only just beginning for the working wife and mother. Bogged down with the daily rituals of domesticity, such as cooking, doing dishes, bathing children and scrubbing floors, the illusion of the cozy home quickly fades. Many working women complain, "It is the same thing every day." When they come home from work, their sinks and countertops are piled high with dirty dishes from the night before, their clothing and personal items are scattered about, their bathroom is filthy, and the rest of their home looks as if it has not been attended to in weeks.

The main problem appears to be that working women have so little time for leisurely pursuits. They commute home after work, pick up their kids from day care, prepare dinner and clean up. By eight-thirty or nine o'clock they are ready for bed. When the weekend finally arrives, instead of enjoying a meaningful activity that they are interested in, they spend Saturday and Sunday trying to catch up with cleaning, laundry, and other duties. Committed to a series of agonizing chores they detest, weekends seem almost nonexistent. If they do find the time to go out, by ten o'clock they are exhausted and ready to call it a night. Caught in a vicious cycle of getting up, going to work, coming home tired, preparing meals and performing chores—day after day—many women feel trapped. Unchanging and inescapable, their routine imprisons them. All they want to do is run away from the stress.

Household Management

Even though the perpetual task of maintaining the home can seem hopeless, there is a solution: a step-by-step system that will make housework bearable. Women need to approach domesticity with the same proficiency as they would any high-paying professional assignment. First, they should define what needs to be accomplished, set their objectives, and devise a strategy that works for them. Household management is the most efficient way for the professional woman to meet the demands of her busy home. The suggestions mentioned in this chapter are not meant to replace your favorite approach to housecleaning. Instead, these recommendations, if followed, will make the time devoted to maintaining your home much easier.

Sharpen Your Perspective

The best way to find out what makes housework so loathsome is to take a closer look at how you, your roommate, or your family are approaching domestic chores. Set a week aside for you and the other members of your household to do a comprehensive audit. Use this period of time to determine what cleaning schedule works best for you. Do you prefer to clean early in the morning, late in the afternoon, or late at night? Do you like to work alone or as part of a team? Identify the work conditions you prefer best. Notice which chores are a complete waste of your time. Write down all your observations. Have others who are living in the home make their own notes on how their work habits can be improved. At the end of the week, call everyone in the home together and have a meeting to discuss their observations and suggestions.

Make up a cleaning schedule for each room in the house to determine how often it should be cleaned. List the function of the room and how much activity transpires there. This will help you to access daily, weekly, and quarterly cleaning specifications and to eliminate all unnecessary overcleaning. Learn to budget your time. Give top priority and diligence only to rooms that get the most traffic. Whenever possible, try to get away with spot cleaning. Less noticeable areas can be attended to when your schedule is not as demanding or on a bi-weekly, or even monthly, basis. Give top priority to tasks that, once completed, will benefit you and your family the most. Never start cleaning in the kitchen or the bathroom. These rooms take the longest to clean and they will end up depleting all of your energy. Another good reason to hold off on these areas until last is that they tend to get dirty again in the process of cleaning the rest of the house. Start with rooms that have less furniture and are less cluttered, such as the den, living room, or entrance hall. Move on to rooms that have less everyday activity in them, such as the guest room, dining room and bedrooms.

Make sure when you set housekeeping goals that you allow enough time to do them. Creating deadlines is important, but time schedules must be realistic. If you plan to do too many chores in too short a time you will become overwhelmed. On the other hand, if you allow too much of a time cushion you may become distracted and may procrastinate. Never allot more time than is needed to complete a specific task. Otherwise it will drag on and turn into drudgery.

One of the main reasons why people hate housecleaning so much is because it is so tedious. If you find that a particular task is becoming tiresome, try going about the chore in a different way. For example, change the location where you are working, approach another aspect of it, or stand instead of sitting. The trick is to stimulate your mind to keep from becoming restless and bored. Be inventive; it will free you from the uniformity of domesticity. One creative way to break the monotony of a routine task is to wear a watch to calculate how long it takes you to complete an assignment. Record your speed. Next time, try to break your record by working a little faster.

A task is interesting rather than monotonous to the degree that the process of doing it is enjoyable. Integrate your domestic duties with activities you enjoy, such as watching television, listening to a book on tape, learning a new language, talking on the telephone, or listening to some lively music.

All of us have our less productive days. Certain household chores can be performed at odd times or, if necessary, put off until another day. Learn to be flexible with yourself. Whenever possible, curtail chores to match your agenda, motivation and energy. Tackle the hard chores when you're in a productive mood and work on easier tasks when you are less motivated. Most importantly, learn to listen to your body. Go along with your energy cycle rather than working against it. If you become fatigued, stop and take a short break. Not only will you be more productive when you come back, but you will feel less exhausted, less irritable and less resentful.

Save Time With The Morning Run-through

The best way to keep ahead of your household chores is to practice "preventative housekeeping." At the start of the day, go through each room in your home and double-check it for neatness. Pick up any clutter that is scattered around. Allow no more than five minutes per room for your morning run-through. The only exceptions to this rule should be your kitchen and bathroom. Those rooms could take up to fifteen minutes longer to tidy up. If you come across a task that demands more time, write it down and come back to it later when you can spare the time. Make the morning run-through into a regular habit and you will find yourself with more free time on the weekend.

Be Properly Equipped

Save yourself a lot of frustration by gathering up all the cleaning supplies and equipment you will need before you start the cleaning process. Use a carry-all caddie to transport your cleaning supplies from room to room. Make sure it has a handle and steep sides to prevent supplies from falling out. Another way to keep your supplies at your immediate disposal is to wear an apron while you're cleaning. Sew extra pockets on it to hold debris and cleaning supplies, such as a toothbrush for scrubbing tight, impossible-to-get at-areas; a scraper to remove grime; a feather duster and dust cloth for polishing; and paper towels. Two side loops can be sewn on to hold squirt bottles containing liquid cleanser for countertops, and glass cleaner for windows and mirrors.

A Well-run Home Requires Team Effort

For the working wife or single mother, running the household is a tough little business and the responsibility should not belong exclusively to her. If a woman is working outside the home, she has two jobs. Not only does she put in forty hours at the office but she puts in another forty at home. Homemaking should involve a collaborative effort on the part of everyone living in the household, particularly if children are old enough to help. The family is a unit, with each member an equal part of the whole.

According to Dr. Kevin Leman, in his book *Making Children Mind Without Losing Yours*, "One basic approach to get children to cooperate more with housework is to point out the need for their cooperation in the home." Hopefully, you will be fortunate enough to have children who understand that their participation will ease your workload and, as a result, cut down on your stress.

Whenever possible, let your children be self-governing. No one likes to be saddled with a job they detest doing. It really doesn't matter who does what, as long as everyone recognizes what is expected of them and understands how to perform the job correctly. Be sure to list all of your specifications for an acceptable result beforehand so that children will know exactly what is expected of them. Children cannot learn merely from your example; they need to be trained. If you take time out in the beginning to watch over and to supervise them, it will prevent confusion later on and will keep them from coming back to you for clarification.

Children should be trained in—and should master—all the basic homemaking skills, regardless of their gender. Rotate chores so each child gets to take his or her turn at performing a specific task.

Getting Your Partner To Participate

Couples who maintain comparable work schedules need to find a common approach to the problem of housework. When it comes to handling domestic chores, women tend to push themselves too hard. They overburden themselves with domestic demands and are often victimized in the process.

Even though more men than ever before are demonstrating liberal and progressive attitudes toward housework, there are still men with preconceived notions that regard domestic chores as a woman's work. Despite the fact that women hold full-time jobs outside the home, household tasks such as cleaning, cooking, food shopping, child care, and sewing, are still considered wifely responsibilities. This is most dramatically reflected in the number of domestic arguments that occur over housework. In fact, it is one of the main causes of conflict in a relationship. Outdated gender roles work against career women, forcing them to do double duty. Unlike the job they hold outside the home, housework has no set hours and no holiday or overtime pay.

The career woman's husband or live-in lover is not her enemy. He is not trying to denounce or diminish her worth by not participating in the housework. If anything, he is insensitive to her special needs. More likely than not, his indifference is the result of past programming and old patterns of thinking which no longer apply to the current state of marriage or partnership. One of the problems of this society is that men are conditioned from childhood to fill traditional role models. During the first half of their lives they are taught to be "real men." As a result, they frequently become trapped by primitive behavior, both learned and inherited. Men that are accustomed to having mothers, wives, and secretaries that care for them are bound more by tradition than sensibility. Such men are less likely to help with housework, no matter how overburdened their wives are. They are even more reluctant if they consider the chore women's work. Women sometimes perpetuate this attitude by automatically assuming the role of the self-sacrificing, tireless, uncomplaining and nurturing "little wife."

Husbands and wives must break free from these old stereotypes and work together as equal partners in the home. A happy marriage is never possible without equality. When two people consider one another as equals, gender differences diminish and it becomes easier for them to mutually undertake the responsibilities of managing their home together.

When It's Time For Outside Assistance

If you fail in your attempt to coax your roommate, husband or children into sharing responsibility for household chores, or if you find your leisure time is being consumed by domestic duties, then you may wish to hire a professional housecleaner. Although bringing in outside help is a sensible solution, amazingly, many women are reluctant to do it. One of the reasons they are hesitant is because of ingrained programming that equates cleaning and caring for the home as wifely traits. Women have been taught from a very early age that a good homemaker not only runs her own home but finds her role as housewife personally fulfilling and satisfying. Studies also indicate that another common reason working women are reluctant to hire help is because they are uncomfortable asking other women to do what they believe is demeaning work. Consequently, much of a professional woman's leisure time is spent performing routine household tasks instead of pursuing personal interests or spending time with her husband and children.

Regardless of her reservations, the reality is that the modern woman has everything to gain by engaging household help. As working women begin to recognize what their time is actually worth, they will come to the realization that they are better off paying an efficient housecleaner to do remedial tasks around the house, not only for the sake of their career but, for the other priorities in their personal lives as well. An extra pair of hands can free up a woman's schedule and permit her to spend more "quality time" with her family, friends, or just doing something special that she wants to do.

Working women need to stop lavishing so much of their attention on the physical condition of their home, and start instead to take greater care in the making of a home. Enlisting the aid of a cleaning professional is not as costly as one might think. In fact, it takes a lot less out of the family budget than paying for the consequences of too much self-imposed domestic responsibility.

How To Hire A Housekeeper

Your housecleaner should be managed in the same organized manner as anyone who works for you professionally. You will find that it will be a lot less complicated and, in the long run, a lot less expensive if you locate a housecleaner from a legitimate cleaning company or a professional agency rather than obtaining the name of someone from a friend or relative. In most cases, a cleaning company hires, trains and manages their employees and is completely responsible for Social Security, federal taxes and unemployment taxes. Interview the company or agency on the telephone first. You can also contact the Better Business Bureau to determine if the company has any complaints filed against them.

Chances are that if you do hire a housekeeper without using an agency, the Internal Revenue Service (IRS) will consider the housekeeper your employee. This means you will be forced to comply with both federal and state tax requirements. To find out what your legal responsibilities are and what forms you will need, you can contact the IRS directly at 1-800-424-FORM. For your state requirements you can contact your local labor department or your state employment agency.

Once you have chosen an appropriate candidate, schedule an interview with the housecleaner so that they can see your home and give you an estimate. In your selection process, try to accomplish the following:

Points to Consider in Hiring a Housecleaner

Discuss what you want done and how you want it done. Devise a job description based on the chores you normally do on a weekly or bi-weekly basis.

Ask for a free estimate and get the bid in writing. House-cleaners generally charge by the hour or by the job. If the cleaning professional charges by the job, ask that the requested services be itemized.

Inquire about the housecleaner's breakage policy. If the house-cleaner is employed by an agency, ask if the company has liability insurance to cover any damage done to your personal belongings.

Ask the prospective housecleaner about prior experience and request references from at least one previous customer.

Before making a long-term commitment, ask the house-cleaner to come for only one visit. This will give you an opportunity to judge the work without feeling obligated.

Make a thorough inventory of all your cleaning supplies in advance and stock up on cleaning items that are most frequently used.

Make sure all your cleaning equipment is in top condition. Invest in a good vacuum cleaner, one with superior suction and the proper attachments. Be sure to install a new vacuum cleaner bag on the day the housecleaner arrives and have a spare one on hand.

Be prepared for the housecleaner when he or she arrives. Put away any personal items that may be scattered around. A professional cleaner's job should be to clean, not to pick up personal belongings or work around messy rooms.

Make a list of priceless objects you do not want touched and point them out to the housecleaner before cleaning starts. Put away any personal valuables that may tempt, such as expensive jewelry or money. Do not leave important papers or documents near waste receptacles where they may accidentally be thrown away.

Even if you cannot afford a professional housekeeper on a regular basis, it may be wise to consider getting part-time assistance for major housecleaning chores, such as filthy windows, soiled carpets and greasy walls.

More Help For The Working Homemaker

Pick up a few new housekeeping tips from The Clean Team, a group of cleaning professionals who clean entire homes in only forty-two minutes. Learn their method from their book *Speed Cleaning* by Jeff Campbell and you will work smarter and faster. You can also write or call for their free product catalog:

The Clean Team, 2264 Market Street San Francisco, Ca. 94114 (415) 621-8444.

CHAPTER 7

The Crucial Role of Friendship

*I*nvolving friends in one's life is essential to well-being. Aside from the care and support they provide, we need friends to laugh and play with. Their presence in our life is vital for our mental and physical health. Friends encourage us to express our needs, define our troubles, and ventilate our inner emotions. A good friend can multiply the experience of joy and lessen the pain of loss. The bond that links us to a friend is not one of blood, but of mutual respect and joy in each other's life.

Maintaining or establishing new friendships is not easy for a woman who is preoccupied with her career and is already barely able to cope with all the pressures of her busy life. The drive for success, independence, financial status, and material improvement can greatly interfere with personal relationships. The inability to find the time to socialize is a commonplace predicament many women today find themselves struggling with. For the professional woman there are times when it seems as if there are not enough hours in her day. Friendships slowly slip away as she uses up her allotted time off to catch up on office work, run errands or complete household chores. Lack of energy and exhaustion brought about by excessive demands can deplete the stamina of even the most energetic of women. Regardless of how our jobs or busy lifestyles interfere with our attachments to others, we must make a conscious effort to form and maintain close friendships. Loneliness and isolation need not accompany success.

Too often, in the working world, women substitute business contacts and networking for friendship, often unaware that their real friendships are gradually drifting away. Late at night when the emotional support of a real friend is required, they come up empty. No one is there to listen to their problems or their deepest fears.

It does not take long to learn that business contacts and co-workers make poor substitutes for real friends. While it is wonderful if the professional woman can form a close relationship with someone she works with, a woman who is serious about her career knows she must be careful about sharing intimate details about her private life with an associate at the office. Revealing private details about one's family, love life or personal finances to a colleague can later prove embarrassing. If for any reason this close relationship is dissolved, the one that knows all can share these intimate details with others and the career woman could become the object of office gossip or ridicule.

For a woman to be truly successful in both career and personal life, she needs the companionship of others outside the work environment. In particular, she has a need to relate to someone on a more intimate level and freely express to someone her inner emotions. Friends can offer us comfort, diversion, intellectual stimulation, and even a deeper insight into ourselves. They can play a crucial role in our development. Each of us is a unique individual and there are many parts to our personality. Different people bring out different sides of us. A friend need not be a person that shares our same desires, has our same ambition, income, or even background. Our friendships permit us to experiment with the various components of our personality. Sometimes we make friends with the type of person we would most like to be, or by being around one who is so different from ourselves that we can mirror our fantasies and live vicariously through them.

For many of us, the image we have of ourselves—rightly or wrongly—is what other people have told us we are. There is a desperate human need to see in someone else's eyes our own value and worth. We learn a lot about ourselves by the way others respond to us. How our friends interact with us helps us determine the causes of our pain or pleasure, and what makes us feel confident or insecure, proud or ashamed about ourselves. Friends offer us the opportunity to find our strengths or change qualities that make us feel uncomfortable with who we are.

The Female World Of Friendship

As children, both boys and girls are encouraged to participate in social gatherings by sharing and cooperating with others. Early on, though, young girls are taught different socialization skills than boys. Unlike young males, who are often brought up to conceal their emotions, most girls are raised to express their feelings and expose their vulnerability. Culturally, it has always been more acceptable for females to be more expressive to one another emotionally and physically than it has been for males. As a result women are endowed with special nurturing qualities, such as sensitivity, tenderness and compassion, that help them relate differently than men do to one another. Women tend to be more good-natured, open and caring. Because women are more willing to reveal intimate parts of their personalities, they have a deeper capacity for friendship. Unlike men, who choose social group activities with casual acquaintances or business associates, most women prefer self-revealing interaction with smaller groups of closer friends...a clear reflection of their intensity of involvement.

Historically, women have been lead to believe that female relationships are inferior to those of men. Sadly, even today, many women still perceive their friendships with other women as frivolous and superficial.

Unfortunately, some women fail to see the greater significance of friendship with the same sex. So important is the friendship between women, in fact, that middle-aged or older women that lack female friends sometimes succumb to serious psychological problems.

Women as Friends

Women turn to one another for a variety of reasons: self-definition, empowerment, sharing their career victories and defeats, acceptance and reassurance, help in sorting out the difficulties in each other's lives, evaluation of their relationships with men, comforting of each other and alleviation of emotional suffering from abandonment.

Too often, women feel that their female worth or prestige depends on their attachment to men, thereby making their female relationships secondary. Most women admit that praise means a lot more to them if the compliment comes from a man. Traditionally, women are taught to compete with each other for the attention of men. Brought up to find their identity in men, they weigh themselves against other females, their rivals for these favorable male sources of sanctuary.

Men have greater importance and status in the world. Women will readily choose the companionship of a man over that of a close female friend (who was merely a fill-in companion) because they believe the man holds the power. What woman cannot recall a time when a girlfriend canceled an engagement with her at the last minute, just to accept an invitation from a man? From early on, women have come to accept second place without question. In many female relationships, it is clearly understood that if a man asks either one of them out on a date, a date with a man takes top priority over any plans they may have made previously.

In order to enrich our friendships with women, we need to stop using each other as substitute companions. We need to rethink our habitual responses toward our own sex and place a much higher regard on the importance of female companionship in our lives. Women need to take pride in the fact that they are better than men in relating intimately. This distinction is why men so often will expose their vulnerability to a woman rather than to other men, in some instances even the closest of their male companions.

No woman should ever expect a man to fulfill all her emotional and social needs. Female friendships are necessary even if women are involved in intimate relationships or are married. Cultivating strong friendships with other women reduces the desperate dependence some women occasionally place on the men in their lives. No one can be everything to any one person. Many of the things women find interesting are viewed by men as "senseless" and "dull," such as decorating, entertaining, cooking, current fashion trends and shopping. When asked, most women admit they feel more relaxed in the company of another woman because they do not have to be as concerned with their physical appearance. Women share a very special bond with one another, a camaraderie that we do not have with the men in our lives. We need each other for moral support and for the depth and intensity only female friendships can provide.

Maintaining Friendships

Friendship is a matter of choice. It is not based on blind allegiance or given unequivocally. The deep emotional connection that exists in friendship must be nourished; it will not exist on mere memories, on what once was. The quickest way to end a friendship is to neglect it. We must be careful to filter in new ideas and experiences and not be careless and inattentive to those we call our friends. Effort is required on the part of both parties if the friendship is to continue.

The strength of the friendship will vary at times depending on the particular needs of the individuals involved in the relationship. Close friends should connect up to two times a week to discuss the mundane details and the incredible events of their everyday lives, occurrences that might otherwise be forgotten with less frequent contact.

Twelve-Point Guide to Healthy Friendships

1. Be careful not to overburden your friend with your problems and anxieties.

2. Learn to be a good listener. Refrain from offering advice or moralizing.

3. Respect your friends point of view. Different personalities can complement each other. It is not always necessary that you see eye to eye.

4. Clear up misunderstandings as they arise. If you feel exploited by your friends actions, communicate your feelings immediately. Harboring negative thoughts leads to hostility.

5. Let differences pass; there is no sense in rehashing old arguments.

6. Never "fill" idle periods with your friend's company. Instead, set aside special time for the development of the friendship.

7. Never betray a trust. Trust, when violated, can ruin even the best friendship.

8. Bring competitiveness out in the open. Men do not allow it to interfere with their relationships; why should women?

9. Never compete for the attention of your friend's love interest. Doing so is not really proof of your own desirability.

10. Support and praise your friends; ignore failures and imperfections.

11. Never resent a friend's success. Strive to admire his or her achievements instead.

12. Accept the kindness of a friend. Allow friends to do things for you, too.

Letting Go Of Friendship

The type of friends we need will vary over the course of our lifetimes. Establishing new friendships is often necessary when a woman advances herself; her attitudes about who she is and how she views life change as she takes on a new identity. Even her oldest and dearest friends may become strangers. They may not understand the pressures of her new lifestyle; or she may feel as if she has very little in common with them. In order for a friendship to be ongoing, each person must affirm the other's individual worth.

Sometimes we lose contact and are separated from friends because of external forces: we change jobs or are forced to move. But, regardless of external circumstances, the ties of friendship cannot be severed unless there are internal problems to begin with.

When Is It Time To End A Friendship?

When friends no longer meet each other's needs. When frequent arguments arise that involve nasty insults, recriminations, accusations, and criticism. When friends reject and disrespect each other's point of view. When one or both friends refuse to structure time to spend together. When one person encounters a personal crisis and begins to rely on the other in a new, more demanding way.

Meeting New People and Making New Friends

Old friendships should be balanced with new ones. Entertain the possibility of making friends with persons of diverse interests, ages and backgrounds. If we do not make new friendships as we advance through life, we will soon find ourselves alone and isolated. Every day we come in contact with all sorts of people, but if we are preoccupied with emotional problems, we are not fully aware of those around us. We grow emotionally and intellectually by relating to others. Every new contact we make is an open invitation to learn something new about life.

There is a skill to developing deep, meaningful relationships with others. It starts with a genuine affection toward people. Individuals that are well liked and that get along well socially take an active interest in others. Instead of always trying to attract attention to themselves, they are fascinated by other people. They take time to listen intently to what others have to say. They draw people out of their shell by asking them questions about their interests. Human contact is a challenge. Making new friends requires imagination and the capacity to appreciate people and all their complexities. It means risking self-exposure and revealing our inner selves to another. To make new friends we must be open, honest, natural and sincerely interested in the lives of others.

Qualities People Look For and Respect in Others

In seeking friends, we look for enthusiasm, good sense of humor, ability to communicate feelings, ability to take criticism, willingness to compromise, empathetic nature and reliability.

There is an unlimited number of exciting people around you who, when you get to know them, may become life-long friends. The best way to meet new people is to pursue what you enjoy doing, what stimulates and motivates you. Attend a lecture on a favorite subject or take a class in it. Spend time engaging in activities that involve your interest. Sign up for a retreat, or volunteer. You will be surrounded by people who have something in common with you.

Where to Make New Contacts

Start focusing your attention on others at social or recreational events and even on people in your own neighborhood. Go out of your way to engage in new, potential contact activities. In social situations, be alert to individuals whose grooming and body language suggest that they are approachable. The following gestures indicate a positive response: a smile, direct eye contact, uncrossed arms and legs, a nod of the head and leaning forward to hear what is being said. Allow your posture to say you are open and receptive, too. Extend your hand first, smile, and introduce yourself. Begin a casual conversation and signal your interest in getting to know them better. Suggest an informal meeting, to become better acquainted. Select a date and exchange telephone numbers. Just before the scheduled meeting, call to confirm and let them know you are looking forward to seeing them again. Be honest about your expectations for the friendship from the outset, but be careful not to rush the friendship by revealing intimate details about your life. Allow the friendship time to gradually develop. Most importantly: be patient. Friendship takes weeks, months and even years to develop.

$\mathcal{C}$HAPTER 8

Benefits of a Balanced Diet

Statistics indicate that, at any given time, nearly half of all American women are on a diet. In a diet-conscious culture such as ours, where women identify with fashion models the way young men identify with athletes, it is hard for the average woman to measure up to such rigid standards. A recent survey in First Magazine (May 1992) reported that out of five thousand men and women surveyed, 75% of the women had been on a weight-loss diet at some point in their lives. Research concluded that dieting is the norm in the U.S. and that it is driven more by fashion than by health needs.

From early on, young girls are raised to think that they can grow up to look like the model on the cover of their favorite fashion magazine. They are never told that the photograph has probably been retouched or that the cover girl has spent thousands of dollars on cosmetic surgery.

When it comes to physical appearance, women are at a disadvantage. Peer pressure and cultural attitudes lead some women to believe that only "thin is beautiful." As a result, they risk their physical and mental health to attain a flawless figure. They spend half their life trying to measure up to someone else's idea of the perfect woman.

Because of the pressures society puts on women to be thin, few overweight women possess high self-esteem. Every time they see their reflection in a mirror they focus on those extra pounds, interpreting each bulge as a physical confirmation of their imperfection.

When it comes to her weight, a woman's fear of becoming fat becomes a full-blown drama. Because today's standard of "thin" means abnormally slender, very few women achieve their ideal weight without great effort. In their obsession to obtain the "perfect body," many women will compromise their health by exercising too much, dieting to excess, inducing themselves to vomit, and abusing diuretics and laxatives.

Women spend a good deal of their time—in fact, too much time—discussing their weight: how much they have gained, how much they have lost, the newest fail-safe diet, liposuction, tummy tucks or which physical activity will burn off the most calories the fastest. Some women become so fixated on their weight that they virtually starve themselves to maintain their shape. In their hurry to lose those extra, unwanted pounds as quickly as possible, they skip meals or cut back on their caloric intake to the degree that they are left light-headed, dizzy and fatigued. Improper eating habits sap women of their strength and vitality and cause long-term health problems. Lack of nutrients in the diet weakens the immune system which can, in turn, increase susceptibility to infections and viruses.

What Is Food?

Food is anything with a chemical composition that can provide the body with material used to produce heat, activity, and other forms of energy. Food is any substance that is eaten, drunk or absorbed that allows the growth and repair of organisms and the maintenance of life.

Very few women watch what food they put into their bodies for the sake of their health. Most are careful about what they eat only because they are afraid of gaining weight. If asked how important their health is, most women would answer, "Health is my number-one priority." Yet, the main reason most women diet to the point that it jeopardizes their health is because their main priority is not, as they say, "their health," but their appearance. Women need to recognize the fact that without good health, nothing else matters.

Eating For Your Health

The only way to have a well-proportioned figure and maintain good health is to eat well-balanced meals. It does take will power to eat wisely and moderately but it is worth it in the long run. Eating properly ensures vitality, peace of mind, a healthy complexion, beautiful hair and nails, and diminishes the possibility of a multitude of health related problems caused by poor nutrition.

Hypoglycemia

Poor nutrition causes disease. Hypoglycemia is a diet related condition that is caused by low blood sugar, commonly diagnosed in women. Some of the mental and physical symptoms related to low blood sugar fluctuations are depression, irritability, fatigue, headaches and poor memory. Lack of the proper nutrients in the diet can also cause nervousness, mental confusion, dizziness, lack of coordination, leg cramps, drowsiness, and insomnia. If you have a history of any of these symptoms and you can relieve them by eating, there is a good chance you have hypoglycemia and should see a physician to be tested. If left untreated, low blood sugar can cause asthma, allergies, peptic ulcers, epilepsy and even cancer. A common prescription for hypoglycemia is a high-protein, low-carbohydrate diet program that includes frequent snacking to prevent blood sugar from dropping too low.

When we eat properly, we not only look better, but we feel healthier, both mentally and physically. The only way to insure that we will make the appropriate food choice is to acquire nutritional wisdom through self-education. A successful eating program starts out with common sense and a background on what foods will furnish the basic nutrients our bodies need. Just in case we have overlooked any essential vitamins or minerals in our diet, it helps to have an idea of what multivitamin supplements we should take.

Vitamins

In a fast-paced, demanding world such as ours, it is often difficult to take the time to care and nurture ourselves the way we should. Our body, however, has certain nutritional requirements that must be met in order to safeguard our health. Wholesome eating habits reduce the risk of contracting diseases and are the best defense against the stress of everyday living.

Sound nutrition demands that all the important nutrients be eaten every day. You can get most of the vitamins and minerals you need from a well balanced eating program. It should consist of foods chosen from the following six major food groups: milk, fat, protein, grains, vegetables and fruit. Protein helps form antibodies that fight infection, supply you with energy and help build and repair body tissues. Fat supplies energy, helps your body absorb fat-soluble vitamins, and supplies essential fatty acids. Carbohydrates, such as pasta, rice, whole grains, lentils, peas and dried beans, add fiber to your diet and promote endurance. Fruits abound with nutrients that increase resistance to disease; vegetables keep the skin healthy and smooth, assist cells in using oxygen and promote the healing of wounds.

Unfortunately, no matter how careful you are about your diet, there is no guarantee that what you eat will provide you with the recommended daily allowances of the vitamins and minerals you need. Dietary supplements replace amino acids, minerals, enzymes and vitamins missing from your diet. They help you digest, store, and convert the food you eat into energy. They also build bones, teeth, genetic material and hormones.

Contrary to popular belief, vitamins cannot replace food. In fact, they can not be assimilated without ingesting food. They are not pep pills and have no caloric nor energy value of their own. If you were to stop eating food and take only vitamins, you would seriously threaten your health.

To determine what nutritional supplements you need, check with your physician; only he will know your health profile and is the best to judge what nutrient therapy will be most beneficial.

The Importance Of Fiber In The Diet

It is believed that constipation leads to irritation of the cells of the colon and can possibly produce cancer. A diet rich in fiber helps speed up elimination, which pushes food through the body more rapidly, thus reducing obesity. Fiber will reduce the caloric consistency of your food diet and will slow down the rate at which calories are ingested. It will also reduce your desire to eat as much.

The National Cancer Institute recommends that Americans eat about one ounce of fiber per day. Fiber is classified into two groups: "soluble" and "insoluble," each with its own healthful advantages. Soluble fiber, which breaks down in water, helps to lower cholesterol, stabilize blood-sugar levels, and reduce fat absorption. It is primarily found in oat products such as oatmeal. Insoluble fiber, which does not dissolve in water, helps prevent constipation, gall-stones, hemorrhoids, and a digestive disorder called diverticulosis. It is most commonly found in whole wheat products.

To add more recommended fiber to your diet, increase your intake of whole grain foods (bulgar, buckwheat, cracked wheat flour and bread, whole wheat flour and bread, brown rice, wild rice, and wheat germ). Be sure to read labels on packages. Make sure that you read the word whole or unprocessed in front of rye or wheat. Wheat flour, for example, means the product has been refined.

Raw vegetables are also a good source of fiber, specifically artichokes, beets, onions, parsley, radishes, sauerkraut, tomatoes, squash, eggplant and raw cabbage.

Pod vegetables and legumes also supply fiber to the diet. Select from green beans and peas (fresh or dried), lentils or lima beans.

Seeds and unsalted, dry-roasted nuts are also high in fiber content. Fruit is another prime source of fiber. Select fruit with tough skin, such as apples, dates, figs, grapes, pears, all varieties of berries and watermelon.

Salt

Sodium causes retention of watery pounds. The desire for salt is an acquired taste, not a natural one. We develop our craving for salt in our diets during infancy because so many brands of baby foods are heavily salted. Too much salt in the diet can cause hypertension, kidney problems, stroke, heart disease, and, in women, premenstrual anxiety, water retention and stress. The American diet contains shocking amounts of salt. Instead of using salt, try herbs, spices, pepper, onions, garlic, lemon and lime juice to enhance the flavor of unappetizing foods.

High Sodium Foods. Certain vegetables and seafood contain high amounts of sodium and should only be consumed in moderation.

Vegetables

Artichokes	Celery
Chard	Spinach

Seafood

Crab	Herring
Salmon	Sardines
Scallops	Shrimp

Low Sodium Foods. The following are just a few of the many low-sodium vegetables and fruits you should consider for your daily diet.

Vegetables

Asparagus	Onions
Cucumber	Peas
Eggplant	Tomatoes
Green Beans	Zucchini
Green Peppers	

Fruits

Apples	Cherries
Apricots	Peaches
Bananas	Pears
Blackberries	Pineapple
Blueberries	Watermelon

Natural Diuretics

Diuretics are medications that withdraw water from the body. They are generally administered by diet doctors to patients to speed up weight loss. They stimulate the kidneys to draw water from the blood and excrete it in the urine. Unlike chemicals used, natural diuretics will not create negative side effects such as dehydration, nausea, or drowsiness. What they do is dislodge fatty deposits that accumulate and adhere to adipose cells. Natural diuretics locate and destroy fatty deposits by breaking them down, pushing them through the body and eliminating them. Here are some of the natural diuretics you can use:

Apple Cider Vinegar . . .two tablespoons in a glass of cold water per day

Asparagus . . . . .prepare fresh, short cook, stir-fry or lightly steam

Beets . . . . .eat raw

Brussels Sprouts . . . . .short cook, steam

Cabbage . . . . .eat raw, steam or drink the juice

Carrots . . . . .drink the juice, shred, or steam

Cucumbers . . . . . . .eat raw

Lettuce . . . . .the darker the lettuce leaves, the more nutrients they contain

Onions . . . . .a raw onion should be eaten every day, either sliced or shredded

Radishes . . . . .eat raw

Tomatoes . . . . .drink the juice (make sure it is sodium-
free), slice or stew.
Calcium tablets   . . . . .will help reduce water retention

Sweet Suicide

Our attraction to sweet substances begins as children. Many baby foods and formulas contain sugar. Because eating habits are formed in childhood, by the time we reach adulthood many of us are permanently addicted to sugar and have serious sugar habits.

Sugar addiction is a worldwide phenomenon. Sugar, like alcohol and tobacco, is a substance for which people rapidly develop a craving. Because of its many forms, sugar is not addictive the way narcotics are, but constant ingestion can lead to psychological and physiological dependency.

Sugar is converted into glucose by the body's digestive juices and is carried through the bloodstream to the pancreas, which is stimulated into producing insulin. Ingesting an excessive amount of sugar overstimulates the pancreas into producing an excess of insulin. This frequently leads to an addiction to sweets that satisfy the insulin secretion.

Although sugar does raise your blood sugar level temporarily, within a short time your body will use it up and you will be left with one or several of the following symptoms of low blood sugar: headache, dizziness, fatigue or irritability. The only relief is to reach for another sweet and repeat the process.

The importance of our daily diet becomes apparent when we stop to think that what we eat is converted into living body cells. To maintain our health we must eat properly. Unfortunately, almost half of the American diet consists of refined carbohydrates (refined sugar, white flour, pastas, polished rice, and refined cereals). As we become more dependent on processed foods, we are consuming more refined sugar than any other previous generation. We have become a nation of sugar addicts. Sugar is in almost everything we eat. Most supermarket food labels attest to the fact that it is practically impossible to escape sugar. Sugar is not only found in obvious foods such as candies and pastries. It is also found in canned beverages and foods, sauces, frozen vegetables, dried fruits, roasted nuts, luncheon meats, ketchup, salad dressings, cheese, TV dinners and almost all "convenience foods."

A diet rich in sugars and starches and inadequate in proteins, vitamins, and minerals, especially calcium, leads to tooth decay. Sugar adheres to the teeth and forms a perfect medium for bacteria; it feeds the bacteria normally found in the mouth and causes it to multiply. When the bacteria multiply they produce an acid that dissolves the enamel and dentine that teeth are made of. Bacteria also attack the gums and bones that support them.

Tooth decay is not the only damage sugar can do to the body. Recent studies indicate that excessive intake of sugar may also contribute to heart failure. It has been traditionally believed that an excessive intake of animal fats and cheese was the main reason why people contracted heart and artery diseases. Now, new evidence suggests that there is a relationship between coronary disease and sugar.

Constant ingestion of refined sugar retards the body's ability to eliminate waste, which can result in constipation. It drains and robs the entire body of vitamins, minerals, and enzymes by requiring the body to digest, detoxify and eliminate it. Constipation is one of the contributing causes of gall bladder stasis, liver complaints and other digestive disturbances. The results of scientific studies also link diabetes, hypertension, hypoglycemia and even cancer to sugar consumption. Continued irritation caused by improper digestion can cause cancerous lesions to develop in the colon. It has been proven that a high sugar diet is a major contributor to serious diseases and health problems. Eliminating sugar from the diet and restricting the intake of high-cholesterol foods will help reduce the chance of contracting a host of ills.

The next time you are tempted to reach for a mouth-watering, sugary-sweet treat, remember that eating refined sugar carries with it the very real danger of serious health problems in the future. Read labels. Do not be fooled by ingredients such as corn syrup, sucrose, glucose, and dextrose that disguise sugar. Instead, get sugar from natural sources, such as fresh, whole fruits, and free yourself from the physical and psychological effects of sugar.

Aromatherapy

As one alternative to eating, aromatherapy expert Ann Berwick recommends that you explore the use of scent as an appetite appeaser. When hungry, try inhaling a bouquet of fennel, bergamot, orange, grapefruit, juniper, or lavender. You can dab these oils on a hankie, bathe in them or massage them into your body.

Nutritional Guidelines

The best way to balance your weight and at the same time maintain your health is to familiarize yourself with the foods that provide the most nutrients for the calories they cost.

It is recommended that you eat foods in the following categories:

Meat, Poultry and Fish

Liver	Crab (steamed)
Tuna (water-packed)	Haddock
Swordfish	Snapper
Salmon	Chicken
	(roasted, broiled or stewed)

These protein sources will provide the essential nutrients without the high calories.

Dairy Foods

Buttermilk	Nonfat milk
Skim milk	Non-creamed cottage cheese
	Yogurt

Products made from skim milk have the most nutrients and the lowest caloric content.

Grains

Bran flakes	Wheat germ
Whole wheat bread	Pasta (made from whole-wheat)

These grains provide your diet with the daily allowances of essential nutrients.

Fresh Vegetables

Beet greens	Broccoli
Cabbage	Kale
Sweet peppers	Watercress

These vegetables have the highest concentration of nutrients and the lowest amount of calories for their nutritional content.

Fresh Fruits

Apples	Bananas
Berries	Cantaloupe
Grapefruit	Oranges
Pineapple	Pears
Tomatoes	Watermelon

25 Simple And Universal Dietary Suggestions

To maintain stamina and ensure good health, sound nutrition is essential. If you apply these simple guidelines to your dietary habits, you will not believe the difference in the way you look and feel:

1. Eat three meals a day.

2. Never skip breakfast.

3. Allow yourself twenty to thirty minutes for mealtimes. Pace yourself; put your fork down between bites.

4. Avoid talking on the phone, reading, or watching television while eating.

5. Refrain from eating in between meals. If you must snack, eat only fruits and vegetables.

6. Avoid fat and reduce your intake of high-cholesterol foods.

7. To minimize your exposure to any one particular food additive, eat a wide variety of nutritious foods.

8. Try to avoid processed foods.

9. Restrict your choices of meat. Make sure meat is lean and limit yourself to no more than two servings per day.

10. Limit fruit. Eat only two to three servings per day because of sugar content.

11. Refrain from eating too many dairy products (no more than two servings per day).

12. Avoid meat drippings, gravies, bacon, butter, lard, oil (except for canola or olive oil) and cream sauces.

13. Use behavior modification techniques, such as deep breathing, to suppress your desire to binge.

14. Keep track of your weight.

15. Never shop for groceries when you're hungry.

16. Whenever possible, buy fresh vegetables and fruit; avoid purchasing them canned or frozen.

17. To help maintain the vitamins in fresh produce, do not wash fruits or vegetables until you are ready to eat them.

18. Do not overcook vegetables or they will lose their nutrients. Steam, microwave, or stir fry them until they are tender but still crisp.

19. Use salt-free seasonings, lemon, garlic, onion, or add extra flavor to foods by using fresh herbs for seasoning.

20. Avoid foods made with sugar and your appetite for sweets will diminish.

21. Alcohol is high in calories and low in nutrients. Control your intake or refrain completely from drinking liquor.

22. Remember the key to controlling your weight and to maintaining good health is to practice moderation.

23. Maintain your shape or get into a regular exercise program. You will feel more confident about yourself, have more energy, and feel far less stressed out.

24. Drink plenty of water. At least six eight-ounce glasses per day. In the warmer seasons or if you exercise you will need to drink more to fulfill your body's fluid requirement. If you do not like the taste of tap water, drink salt-free seltzers, bottled spring water, mineral water, sparkling water or invest in a water purifier for your home or office.

25. To ensure that you are getting all the vitamins and minerals you need if you are under stress, take a vitamin and mineral supplement. The best time for taking supplements is after meals. If you take your vitamins all at once, take them after the largest meal of the day (at dinner, not breakfast). Be sure to take minerals and vitamins together.

CHAPTER 9

Benefits of a Good Night's Sleep

*I*nsomnia is becoming a common problem among professional women. Studies indicate that one out of every three
adults has trouble falling asleep at night. Women need sufficient rest to function properly. Sound sleep restores the body and
the mind. Poor quality sleep makes it nearly impossible to fulfill day-
to-day obligations, pursue work, and enjoy social interests. Life
becomes a chore when we have to struggle just to stay awake.
Drowsiness interferes with even the simplest of tasks. Frequent mistakes, lack of attention, forgetfulness and lethargy are all indications
of insufficient sleep.

Sleep deprivation brings about irritability, irrationality, hallu-
cinations, mental derangement and, in extreme cases, even death.
Sleep disorders are numerous and varied. Sleeplessness can be brought
about by hundreds of causes, ranging from noise on the street to frequent need to urinate during the night. Difficulty in sleeping should
not be passively accepted. This chapter investigates the significance of
sleep and how a good night's sleep will help you to manage your
waking life better. Whether you suffer from chronic fatigue or occasionally have trouble sleeping, the following self-help routines should
prove beneficial in assisting you to fall asleep and stay asleep.

How Much Sleep Do We Need?

Our need for sleep is individual. Some of us require more of
it than others. Each of us has our own natural mode of sleeping and
waking based on our daily rhythm cycle. The need for sleep naturally decreases with age. For example, a one-year-old baby requires
about fourteen hours of sleep per day. A child of five needs about
twelve hours, and adults need about six to eight hours. As we age,
our ability to sustain sleep declines. This explains why the elderly get
less sleep at night than young adults do. Only *you* can determine how
much sleep you require to feel rested and alert.

What Causes Sleep

It is unknown what exactly triggers sleep. One theory is that there is a reduction in the amount of oxygen that reaches the brain which, in turn, diminishes impulses to the conscious centers. It is also believed that specific cell groups throughout the brain bring about sleep when stimulated.

We sleep not only because the body needs to rest but because the brain needs to dream. Memory, the ability to react quickly, and other intellectual functions improve when we get a good night's sleep.

There are two kinds of sleep: "slow-wave sleep" and "dreaming sleep." Slow-wave sleep is a dreamless state. It starts the sleeping sequence. Dreaming sleep is the second stage, also known as REM (rapid eye movement) sleep. It is during REM sleep when most vivid dreams take place. The two sleep states alternate throughout the night. Studies have shown that when REM sleep is interrupted, we react by feeling nervous and tense. REM dream cycles, not sleep itself, are what refresh the mind.

Why We Dream

Sleep may revive our bodies, but it is our dreams that restore our minds and discharge our tensions. Dreaming enables our brains to sort through all the new information we receive during the day. Our culture requires us to continuously suppress many of our natural urges. It is believed that when we dream, our subconscious acts out many of our hidden fears and anxieties. The brain works in much the same way as a computer, acting up on programmed instructions. When we sleep these commands are reduced. Dreaming allows us enough time to process new information, review it, change it or reject it.

Dreams enable us to work through many of our problems. In our dreams we examine situations that we may refuse to recognize consciously. A dream may be cheerful or gloomy, uplifting or distressing, scary or reassuring. Dreams may warn us of impending dangers or troubles, or emphasize pleasant experiences. Dreams of significance are generally more vivid and clear, as opposed to those that are vague or hazy.

Suggestions To Promote Relaxation and Sleep

Exercise

The grogginess we sometimes confuse with physical fatigue can be dispelled with exercise. If you are confined to an office, get out on your lunch hour and take a brisk ten-minute walk. Being inactive and breathing stale air all day long can make you feel weary. Walking is a great way to renew energy. It provides a boost to circulation and can help reduce anxiety by defusing tension. Try to exercise regularly. If done continually, even moderate exercise will improve muscle tone and cardiovascular fitness. Scientists claim that a thirty-minute walk, before or after dinner, will also help you to sleep better at night.

The American Medical Association reports that strenuous exercise will have a more beneficial effect on sleep if it is performed in the late afternoon rather than in the morning. If you have had a particularly hard day, try doing a series of stretching exercises just before bed. They will ease that "uptight" feeling of pressure and help sedate you, making it easier for you to drift off to sleep.

Soak In An Herbal Bath

A bath can become a tranquilizer and sleep inducer. When added to the bath water, scented oils produce delightful aromas and are relaxing to distressed spirits. A couple drops of the following essential oils added to your bath water are recommended: ylang ylang, neroli, marjoram, lavender, sage, and camomile. For information on ordering pre-made essential oils, contact: Atelier Esthetique Institute of Esthetics, Inc., 386 Park Ave. South, Suite 1409, New York, NY 10016 (800) 626-1242.

The temperature of the bath water is the most important factor. An inexpensive water thermometer can be used to monitor and control water temperature. Keep the water at 100 degrees Fahrenheit. Soak a towel in cold water and roll it up to use as a cushion on which to rest your neck. Make sure that your entire body is submerged up to your chin. Stay in the water for at least ten minutes.

Recipe for herbal bath. Steep one-half tablespoon each of rosemary and lavender in one cup of cider vinegar. Add one-quarter teaspoon of either camphor or mint extract. Let this mixture stand for one hour, then add it to your bath water.

Massage

The areas of the upper body such as the face, neck and scalp will provide the most relaxation to the body if massaged at bedtime.

Facial massage. Start off your self-massage by gently running your fingers over your face. Massage your forehead with the balls of your fingertips in a slow, circular motion. Rub sideways, smoothing over your eyebrows with your index and third finger until you reach your temples.

Rest your middle and fourth fingers over your temples and gently vibrate. Slide your hands down to the top of your cheeks, guiding them inward toward your nose. Flatten out your index and third finger and slowly glide them up the sides of your nose until your hands form a steeple at the bridge of your nose.

Again using the balls at the tips of your index and third fingers, smooth over your brows and repeat the circle until you are orbiting the eye area several times.

Now slide your hands down to your lip area. Place both hands side by side over your mouth until your middle fingertips touch.

Then separate your index and third fingers until your lips are exposed. Slide your hands off to the sides of your face and repeat this movement several times.

Place your hands at the base of your throat, overlapping them and laying them flat over your neck. Gently glide the first hand upward until it reaches your chin. As you slide your hand forward under your chin, have the second hand waiting to repeat the movement, again starting at the base of the neck.

Scalp massage. Separate the fingers of both hands and place the balls of your fingers at the top of your scalp. Then slowly guide them back as if you were combing your hair with your fingers. Apply medium pressure. Repeat this movement several times. Let your head fall forward. Starting at the base of your hairline, separate the fingers of both hands and, using the balls of your fingers, glide them forward as if you were still combing through your hair. Repeat this movement several times. Now, using light, circular movements, massage your entire scalp with the tips of your fingers.

For more information on do-it-yourself massage techniques to relieve muscular tension and stress, read Philip Goldberg's and Daniel Kaufman's book, *Natural Sleep*, published by Rodale Press, 33 E. Minor St., Emmaus, PA 18098-0099 (215) 967-5171.

Share Your Stress

Almost everyone, at one time or another, loses sleep over life's ordeals. Talk things over with a friend or family member. Most of us know only a handful of individuals that we can really trust. Call a friend who will listen to your problems and who will comfort you. It should be someone to whom you can disclose sensitive, personal information about yourself without hesitation. Remember, when asked to return the favor, do what you can.

Listen to Soft Music

Soothing music can transform your mood and ease tension. Oliver Wendell Holmes once said, "Take a music bath once or twice a week, and you will find that it is to the soul what the water bath is to the body." Lend yourself to the power of the music and feel it work magic.

Curl Up With A Good Book

Almost all causes of sleeplessness are connected with nervous tension. If you are living under conditions of great strain, curling up with a good book at bedtime will take your mind off your troubles. Reading can be a great way to relax if the material is light.

Cuddle Up to Another Person, Baby or Pet

There is a special feeling that comes from being deeply connected to another life. Hugging makes us feel cozy, safe and protected. Just the act of cuddling itself satisfies, supports, and heals us.

Set The Stage For Comfort

It is important to create a relaxed atmosphere that will promote sleep. Make sure your bedroom is as clutter-free as possible. Clinical studies have shown that a clean room with soft lighting and soothing music, decorated in peaceful colors (such as soft gray, beige, violet and blue), promotes relaxation.

Place a humidifier in your work space during the day and in your bedroom at night. Lack of moisture in the air contributes to higher stress levels. A central humidifier that attaches to your heating unit will keep air moist all winter long. Open windows to circulate air. Sleep with the windows open, weather permitting, whenever possible.

If a room is too cold or too hot it can disrupt your sleep. Adjust the temperature on your bedroom thermostat to somewhere between 60 and 65 degrees Fahrenheit.

When we are asleep we are still aware of certain aspects of our surroundings, such as noises, and bright or flashing lights. Sleep only partially rests the brain; the brain's electrical activity carries on during the sleep state. Wear ear plugs to keep out street noise or purchase a "white-noise" machine. This device is specifically designed to disguise irritating background noise by emitting soothing sounds such as ocean waves, rain, or the hypnotic resonance of a waterfall. The constant hum of a fan or an air conditioner can also be used to mask sounds that interfere with deep sleep.

Darker rooms are more conducive to sleep. If your bedroom is brightly lit, wear eyeshades to shut out the light.

Stop Fretting Over Losing Sleep

Over a period of time, if we are not careful, we can get into the habit of lying awake and worrying about not being able to sleep, instead of actually sleeping. If you cannot sleep, do not allow yourself to become agitated over whether or not you will have enough energy the following day to balance all of your responsibilities. Preoccupation with sleep loss is self-defeating. Refuse to get into that vicious cycle. Discipline yourself to live in the present moment. Instead of worrying about being too tired tomorrow, focus your thoughts on images that will make you feel calm, happy and relaxed. Learn to become peaceful within. Sometimes, we sleep better when we are not expecting to sleep at all.

Think Peaceful Thoughts
To Help Induce Sleep

In order for you to totally relax and have a good night's rest, it is necessary to remove from your mind all the thoughts of the day. Just before sleeping is not a good time to rehash the day's events. Worries concerning business, family, or personal matters can all interfere with our ability to fall sleep.

Refuse to allow dark images of any kind to cloud your mind as you close your eyes and prepare to sleep. Instead, focus your quiet attention on positive images that will calm and soothe you. Take your mind on a mini-vacation. Exchange negative thoughts for positive ones. You can achieve a deep, peaceful feeling by performing any of the following mental exercises. Concentrating on any of these suggestions will help lull you softly to sleep:

a sea gull in flight

the beach at sunset

the reflection of moonlight on a pond

the warm glow of a campfire

a white, fluffy kitten sleeping

drifting off to sleep on someone's lap

floating on a raft in the middle of a lake

foamy, white clouds against a light blue sky

the gentle sound of raindrops on a window pane

being tucked into bed; feeling safe, snug and secure

Don't Let
Your Schedule Get Out Of Control

Another way we miss out on sleep is by scheduling too many activities. Sometimes, without realizing it, we take on too much. We can't stretch time but we can eliminate some of the nonessential events that are squeezed into our daily agenda. Do not shortchange yourself. You cannot continually skimp on sleep or it will show. Squinting, frowning and other strained expressions eventually become permanent if chronic sleep loss persists. Make sure you get enough sleep to look and feel healthy.

Research has concluded that the most important hours for sleep are between 10:00 P.M. and midnight. If you do not get to sleep by then, you will surely experience this sleep loss during the afternoon of the next day (around twelve to sixteen hours later).

Establish A Sleep Schedule

If you go to sleep around the same time each night, you will sleep more soundly. Match your weekend sleep schedule as closely as possible to your bedtime during the week. If you go to sleep later on weekends, and then try to return to your weekly sleep schedule, you may suffer the same symptoms as jet lag.

Things To Avoid
For A Good Night's Sleep

Some people are very sensitive to caffeine. Caffeine can act as a stimulant for up to four hours. Read labels on products that you eat or drink before bedtime. Keep in mind that certain beverages—such as hot chocolate or cola—contain caffeine.

Avoid foods with MSG (monosodium glutamate). In some individuals it produces symptoms similar to those caused by caffeine.

Smoking can cause sleeplessness; nicotine is a powerful stimulant. A survey conducted in England in 1980 concluded that smoking one pack of cigarettes per day reduced sleeping by almost half an hour per night. Studies indicate that heavy smokers that have quit sleep better within only three days.

Avoid napping. Some of us find it hard to sleep because we dose off watching television or reading. Then, when it is time for bed, we have difficulty falling asleep again. Snoozing in the late afternoon or early evening will disrupt your normal sleep and wake cycle and will make it more difficult to sleep at night.

A "nightcap" can prevent sleep. Research data has proven that sleep is found to be generally worse after the consumption of alcohol, even though it may act initially as a sedative by lulling the user to sleep. Alcohol stimulates the production of adrenaline-like neurotransmitters which can interfere with breathing in some persons. When breathing becomes labored, it damages sleep quality. Overindulgence in alcohol can also prevent dreaming. Since dreaming is necessary for our well-being, drinking can deprive us of the opportunity to act out our psychotic tendencies in our sleep. Drinking just before bedtime also increases urine output, which frequently awakens the sleeper with the urge to urinate. Frequent urination interferes with quality sleep.

Refrain from using sleeping pills because they produce a multitude of possible side effects. In some individuals, sleeping drugs actually worsen sleep quality. The sleep state induced by drugs is less deep than normal sleep, with more waking periods that leave the user feeling listless and groggy the next day.

Gaylord Hauser's Recipe
For A Tranquilizing Nightcap

A lack of calcium can be responsible for sleeplessness. Try this warm milk drink to relax your nerves and promote a restful sleep.

Mix one teaspoon of dry skim milk powder in a cup of hot skim milk and flavor with a teaspoon of honey. Sip slowly. For a more tranquilizing affect, some nutritionists recommend taking two calcium tablets with the hot milk. Vitamin B_6 also seems to have a sedative effect on the nerves.

Lettuce Tea

When ingested, the juice of lettuce has a sedative affect on the body. Simply boil the leaves and drink the water as a tea. Those suffering from insomnia claim that it is better than a sleeping pill.

Choose the Appropriate
Sleepwear and Bedding

Sleepwear should be as light in weight as is compatible with warmth; air should be permitted to reach the body. Avoid wearing tight night clothes that bind or bedwear with buttons or bows.

Sufficient bedding is required to provide warmth but not so much as to overheat the body. This can interfere with a good night's sleep. Nylon velour blankets are soft and lightweight, yet incredibly warm; whereas loom-woven wool blankets will provide extra warmth for chilly nights.

Sleep Disorder Centers

If you are suffering from chronic insomnia and you cannot resolve your sleep problems, you should see a physician or contact a clinical sleep disorder center in your area. To locate the closest sleep laboratory, telephone the department of psychiatry at your local medical school or hospital.

CHAPTER 10

The Art of Self-Nurturing

*C*areer women, having been engaged in professional struggles, need to become more engaged in themselves. Time must be found for separateness, for solitude, and for performing beauty-enhancing rituals. These quiet intervals allow for self-renewal at the deepest level. This type of self-acknowledgment is a crucial element of success.

Professional women are judged by others and by the value they place on themselves. When women pay attention to their own appearance, they let others know that they hold themselves in high regard. It is impossible for the career minded woman to promote who she is and what she has to offer if she neglects herself. Very few working women have the energy, intelligence and personality to overcome a negative appearance in their quest for success. Therefore, nurturing ourselves and attending to our needs, both physical and mental, is not self-indulgent. It is impossible to fulfill our responsibilities or to care for others when we do not attend to ourselves first.

When you look your best, and you know you look your best, you feel more confident. Just as the right look can make you feel self-assured, the wrong one can make you feel dowdy. There is nothing worse than being more embarrassed than delighted by the attention you receive. Chipped nail polish, a missing button, a conspicuous stain, or a run in a nylon can strip away your self-assurance. It is difficult to concentrate when you are distracted by a broken bra strap or a sagging hemline. These petty annoyances compete for your attention and lead to distraction. When the details of your appearance have been attended to, your thinking is clearer and more organized.

Importance Of Appearance

Appearance plays more than just a subtle role in the way the business community views professional women. It is not by accident that the majority of successful women are those who make a conscious effort to look their best. Nothing says more about a woman than the way she puts herself together. An attractive, dedicated career woman who has achieved success has, in the process, developed and matured. This, in turn, is reflected in the image she projects. She radiates power. Inevitably, the female professional with a commanding presence wins. Everything about her is purposeful.

If women are not methodical about the way they present themselves in business, they are seriously placing themselves at risk of being interpreted incorrectly. Women who deliberately mastermind their outer image effectively increase their chances of success and greatly reduce the chances of being misunderstood in business transactions.

The Halo Effect

A halo is a circle of light that appears to surround a shining body. The term "halo effect" defines the powerful, psychological influence that our appearance makes upon others during initial contact. This phenomenon occurs from the very first moment we encounter another person; it is the initial impression that we make upon others as a result of our posture, body movements, facial gestures, and clothing.

Studies by Leonard Zunin, M.D., and Natalie Zunin reported in their book, Contact: The First Four Minutes, determined the first four observations that people make when they encounter another person: age, sex, race, and clothing.

This research has also substantiated that social interaction occurs within the first four minutes of an initial encounter. In this brief amount of time, all opinions and assumptions are formulated.

The "halo effect" supports the theory that first impressions make lasting impressions. "Most people are unaware of the meaning and ramifications of those first four minutes," the Zunins write.

"They sense an importance, but they do not realize that we often make or lose contact in that brief initial period."

Playing the Part

From the moment you arrive at your place of work until the time you leave at night, you are on center stage. Like any actress, you have fans and you have critics. If you are a serious-minded career woman, you will want to have as much control as possible over the details of any scene you may be involved in. The "halo effect" stresses the importance of presenting yourself in such a way that it favors the manner in which you will later be perceived by others. Similar to an actress wearing a certain costume that adds authenticity to her role, the career woman must also be specific in the way she packages herself.

Creating the Best Possible You

The purpose of this chapter is to assist you in taking stock of your appearance. It offers suggestions on strengthening your physical presence by identifying your aesthetic needs and the ways in which to meet them. The information it contains can be used to help you explore your current image and to experiment with different options until you find a suitable style that will enhance your personal and professional appearance.

Self-Evaluation

Make a careful study of yourself. Disrobe, stand in the nude, and look into a full-length mirror. View your image as if you were a stranger and you were seeing it for the first time. Each of us has certain parts of our body that we wish we could change. It is probably those areas that are the first to grab your attention. For the purpose of exploring your body effectively, you must look past those areas and allow yourself to become acquainted with your entire body. It is amazing how easily we become emotionally attached to the things we don't like about ourselves and how we take for granted the things that we do like.

We should keep in mind that none of us had a say; we inherited our physical traits at birth. As you observe your physical self, make a mental commitment to like the way you look or, at least, to come to terms with what you have to work with. Vow to make the most of your attributes. One never hears of a successful, attractive woman complaining to others about her shortcomings. She works hard at accepting her entire body with both its flaws and its good points. She refuses to waste her time or energy by bemoaning her imperfections. It is impossible to present a dynamic front to the world when you lack self-assurance. People eventually see through false veneers. A woman who wants to be viewed as being attractive soon realizes that, if she is going to inspire others to see her as such, she must have her own cooperation.

The next time you find yourself focusing on something negative about your appearance, try concentrating on something positive about yourself instead. You will find that you can't think about two things at once.

Posture

No matter how pulled together your look is, poor posture will betray you. Your mannerisms (the ways you walk, sit, and stand) strongly communicate to others how you feel about yourself. When you slouch and slump forward with your shoulders drooping, you appear defeated. However, when you stand erect, hold your head up high, shoulders back and stomach tucked in, you convey confidence by appearing to be more efficient and alert.

Good posture is the proper positioning of the body and the right carriage of the limbs. You will find yourself making a far more forceful impression upon others if you improve this aspect of yourself. Poor posture cannot be adjusted overnight. If you work at it, though, you can re-educate your muscles to behave properly. When practiced daily, the following two exercises will help:

Exercise 1. Align your body by standing with your back against a wall. The back of your head, your shoulders and your buttocks should be touching the wall. Flatten your spine against the wall with your knees bent slightly. The top of your head should be in line with the ceiling. Try to maintain this perfect alignment as you slowly move away from the wall and walk around.

Exercise 2. To maintain the proper posture while seated, sit with the small of your back against the back of a chair and place your feet flat on the floor. Make sure your shoulders are straight and hold your head high. Tuck in your chin and your stomach.

Business Grooming

Today's business environment demands that the career woman's look be carefully planned and coordinated to support her professional standing. There is no greater enemy to a woman's appearance than uncleanliness. After all, who can be attractive with offensive body odor, halitosis (bad breath), dirty hair, problem skin and unmanicured nails? Take care of your physical beauty by taking adequate care of your body.

Personal Hygiene

Cleanliness is one of the most important ways in which you can make a positive first impression. Bathing or showering daily is the best way to diminish anxiety over body odor. After you shower or bathe, you will still need to guard against underarm odor. The regular application of a deodorant or antiperspirant should sufficiently control excess perspiration. Another way to reduce body odor is to remove all traces of underarm hair that hold sweat and bacteria.

Dress shields will absorb moisture and prevent perspiration stains from injuring fabrics and ruining your clothing.

Oxygen, carbon dioxide, fluids and other substances pass in and out of the skin. Clothing should be made from materials that allow air to reach the skin. Also, they should be as light in weight as is compatible with warmth. After a time, certain clothing may collect odors; be sure to discard these garments from your wardrobe.

The professional woman cannot be too casual about womanly odors. The use of feminine deodorants will eliminate rather than merely conceal these embarrassing moments. Such products contain germicidal ingredients that will not harm delicate tissues.

Menstrual flow develops an unpleasant odor when it comes into contact with air. Change pads and tampons often. In addition, you will feel fresher if you use a specially unscented, hygienic powder to mask menstrual odors.

Caring For Your Feet

Foot odor can be controlled by dusting foot powder over your feet, especially between your toes. Sprinkling your shoes with talcum powder before putting them on will keep your feet dry and will help to prevent that sticky feeling.

After a long day, give your sore feet some relief by soaking them in Epsom salts and by massaging them with special cooling creams.

Handling Halitosis (Unpleasant Breath)

Nothing can make you feel more self-conscious in a face-to-face conversation than the threat of having bad breath. While some cases of halitosis are of systematic origin, it is usually attributed to the fermentation of tiny food particles clinging to surfaces of the mouth. Brushing your teeth after meals will prevent bad breath. A travel-size kit containing a toothbrush, toothpaste, and mouthwash can be conveniently stored in your desk.

Be Sensible About Your Scent

Naturally, you'll want to wear a fragrance that is suitable for the office and not one that everyone will notice the minute you walk into the room. A heady "swoon perfume" is too potent an aroma for the workplace. Instead, select a fragile scent that will not offend or nauseate those around you.

Complexion Care

There is only one way to have beautiful skin and that is to learn to properly care for it. Pay a visit to a licensed skin care specialist. Have your skin professionally cleansed and analyzed to determine what products and treatments are suitable for your particular skin type. Many dermatologists now refer to or have aestheticians on staff; ask your doctor for a referral.

Never try to squeeze out a blackhead or a pimple because you could injure blood vessels, infect the area or cause permanent scarring. Medically trained skin care specialists will remove blackheads and whiteheads under the supervision of a physician. They are qualified to answer any number of questions you may have regarding the condition of your skin. Also they will design a simple, no-nonsense skin care regimen that will be easy enough for you to follow. Furthermore, your complexion will undergo a series of changes as the seasons pass. By scheduling quarterly visits, you can modify your skin care regimen to complement the changes in the weather.

Cosmetic Enhancement

Few women take full advantage of what makeup has to offer. A well made up look creates an impact. It gives the career-minded woman an image that says she means business.

Your makeup regimen will depend upon your personal preference, your technical skills, and your time constraints. Makeup is an art; improve your knowledge by investing in a professional makeup lesson. A complimentary makeup session at a cosmetic counter is not a professional makeup lesson and will not provide you with the necessary technical instruction you will need. Only a professional makeup artist with experience can instruct you and design your color palette. Your makeup palette should include shades that support your own natural coloring. Makeup that looks terrific on one woman may look atrocious on another. A well-trained makeup artist will have the capability to study your face and to assist you in making the appropriate cosmetic selections.

Each of us has our own unique concept of beauty. Do not let the makeup artist make all your cosmetic choices for you. Work with this professional. Be very clear on your personal preferences. You may even wish to bring pictures with you to the session of the type of makeup applications you prefer. Try to find photographs of women with your same coloring and bone structure. Watch the application process carefully, ask pertinent questions and take a lot of notes so you can practice later. Makeup, just as with any new skill, must be practiced to be mastered. The more you do it, the faster and more proficient you will become.

Makeup For Work

Elaborate makeup, if worn during daylight hours, can appear theatrical looking. Thick or greasy foundations, brilliant eyeshadow and harsh eyeliner are inappropriate at the workplace. Makeup for the office should be kept to a minimum. Use just enough to even out your skin tone and to enhance your most attractive facial features. Makeup shades should be carefully coordinated to match your own coloring and that of your business attire. To ensure that your application looks natural, always inspect your makeup carefully in daylight before arriving at work.

Makeup After Hours

By intensifying your original application of cosmetics, you can transform your daytime look into a more glamorous evening version. Your eyes and your mouth are the most expressive parts of your face; make sure you give them lots of definition by accentuating them.

Advantages of Arching Your Eyebrows

Eyebrows frame the eyes and add character to the face. Therefore, you should always keep your eyebrows neat. Straggly hairs can give you an untidy look. Well-shaped eyebrows, however, will help to make your face appear more sophisticated. Overly drawn eyebrows can destroy your natural expression and look messy or harsh. Also, be careful if you have considered adding color to your eyebrows. You must select a shade that looks natural and not artificial.

Eyelash tints, brow tints, bronzing gels, or cheek and lip stains can save a lot of time in the morning. Check with your local salon for more information about any of these professional beauty services.

Hair Care

There is nothing as attractive as a beautiful head of hair. So, it is important that it should always be kept immaculately clean. Lubricating conditioners will help to restore body and shine to overprocessed, lusterless hair. For hair to look its best, a good cut is imperative. Damaged hair can result in unmanageable split ends, unless they are trimmed off periodically.

The right hairstyle can create an illusion that can enhance your appearance by adding to or subtracting from the weight of your face. An easy-to-manage hairstyle is more appropriate for a business woman (and is a lot easier to care for) than an ultra-sophisticated style that looks out of place in a work environment. Little-girl hairstyles, such as long hair and pony tails, are inappropriate for the office because they do not project a look of professionalism. The length and style of your hair should be in proportion to your entire torso.

You can add highlights to your natural hair color either by dying it or with chemical-free color treatments. Hair-coloring should only be done by a professional colorist who has the expertise to assist you in selecting the correct shade. Once you have started color treatments, you must maintain them. Nothing will make you look more unkempt than "giveaway roots."

Hand and Nail Care

Many working women neglect their hands. Frequent washing, harsh soaps and hot water will dry out your hands and leave them chapped. A good hand lotion will counteract these ill effects.

The nails of a business woman need to be impeccably groomed because they are always on display. They should be filed down to medium-length or shorter. Improper manicuring, excessive dryness, or paper cuts will cause hangnails. To prevent hangnails, keep your hands and cuticles well moisturized. By rubbing hand cream or lotion into the cuticles several times a day you will accomplish this.

Nail polish can act as a shield to protect the nails. Dark or bright nail polish shades should be avoided unless you want to draw attention to your hands. Select a shade of polish that will not clash with the colors of your outfit.

Maintaining Your Wardrobe

A professional woman's clothing should always be spotlessly laundered, dry-cleaned and wrinkle-free. Take pride in your wardrobe. Regardless of how much your outfits cost, they will not look expensive unless they are kept in good condition. Periodically, go through your closet and examine your clothing for stains, missing buttons, rips, or frayed and sagging hemlines. Rid your closet of tat-tered clothing and outdated styles. Remember to polish your shoes and clean out your purses; if necessary, send them out to be repaired. Finally, you may want to protect your garments from moths by using cedar eggs or blocks.

Career Woman's Basic Wardrobe Plan

A woman's business uniform must be tasteful, appropriate and expressive. Color must be becoming and worn discreetly. Also, the use of decorative accessories should be minimal. In short, all of the elements that contribute to an attractive, well-planned image need to be skillfully combined.

A great wardrobe is the result of a conscious, creative effort. Well-dressed professional women consider the following principles essential: a basic understanding of current fashion trends, simplic-ity, good lines and good fit, originality, proper decorative acces-sories, and matching the suitable clothing with the occasion.

Clothing should project the appropriate image for the work-ing woman, five days a week. Your work costumes should convey authority, power, and position.

Defining Your Unique Style

The following assignment is intended to help you to redesign your current look. It will assist you in defining and expressing your individual sense of style. It will also help to take the fear out of mak-ing future fashion decisions. By the time you finish this exercise, you will have a clear concept of the types of hairstyles, makeup, clothing, jewelry and accessories that appeal to you.

Designing a New Image Workbook

The secret of dressing well is to know the rules of fashion ... and how and when to break them. One of the first requirements of a well-dressed woman is a keen sense of observation and the ability to perceive how clothing and accessories are successfully combined. You will need to collect pictures that illustrate fashion ideas that are especially appealing to you. Obtain as many photographs as you can from European and American fashion magazines and catalogs. Select only those publications containing illustrations of clothing, makeup and hairstyles that interest you and that would fit into your lifestyle. The more variety you have, the more clearly you will be able to discriminate about the fashion looks you prefer. In a short time, you will begin to recognize your personal sense of style by becoming aware of the colors, fabric textures, patterns and designs that appeal to you.

You will need the following supplies:

three-ring binder
index dividers
protective acetate sheets for binder
insertable pocket folders for binder
fashion magazines

Putting Together Your Workbook

Below are the suggested classifications for your binder. As your collection of photographs increases, you may want to make changes or add subdivisions. These pages can be re-arranged or temporarily removed at any time. You will probably want to start with a single binder. Then, you can graduate to a larger size as your workbook expands. Keep all of your pictures organized and ready for instant reference. Continually update your workbook by adding new photographs. This is your private library and an important tool to help you to maintain your unique look. Label all of your pictures according to the category in which you have placed them. This will simplify the process of putting the photos back each time you have used them.

Use index dividers to separate your binder into the following divisions:

Makeup and hairstyles
Leisure and sports-wear
Professional and business look
Formal and evening wear
Materials and patterns
Jewelry, shoes and other accessories
Current fashion information

Place all of the photographs you have selected into the clear acetate folders and file them into their corresponding sections. The insertable pocket folders are for keeping photographs that you may wish to file at a later date.

Makeup And Hairstyles

In this section you will select photographs of models with facial features, bone structure and coloring similar to yours. Select only the photographs of makeup styles that appeal to you.

Next, collect photographs of hairstyles that you like. Remember to choose only the styles that are worn by models with your same face shape. However, it is not necessary for you to select pictures of models with the same hair or skin color as yours. File these photographs in this section as well.

Leisure and Sportswear

This section is designated for illustrations of comfortable fashion looks that you would wear for casual outings or at home. Be on the lookout for photographs of clothing or accessories that you already have. This will present you with a variety of new ideas of how to update your current wardrobe.

Professional and Business Look

Regardless of what you do for a living or where you work, a business look is always a little more formal. Select only fashion looks that you would feel confident being at work with.

Formal and Evening Wear

Again, consider your lifestyle. Look for evening wear that you think would accentuate your assets and minimize your figure problems.

Fabric Materials and Patterns

Now is the time to ask yourself what types of fabrics and patterns you prefer. You are not limited to what you already own; your tastes may have changed. Be daring and consider selecting new patterns and fabrics to wear. (Optional: Visit a fabric store and collect swatches of material for this section.)

Jewelry, Shoes and Other Accessories

Each woman makes her own statement by accessorizing her wardrobe. Accessories should be your individual trademark. They are used to enhance your clothing and to make you look more sophisticated. When you are selecting your photographs of jewelry, pay particular attention to which accessories are in style. Select photos of shoes, stockings, belts, scarves and jewelry.

Clothing That Works

A career woman's life spells activity. Reaching, bending, sitting, standing and walking—all of the motions of the day are made easier by wearing the right clothing. Make sure that your business attire is functional and comfortable.

Take the time to go through your closet and consider each garment carefully. Make a complete inventory to determine if you have the appropriate clothes on hand to accommodate everyday business, special business engagements and dress-up business affairs.

The recommended clothing inventory below will help you to plan your future clothing purchases more carefully. It includes garments that can be purchased on a limited budget, with every article of clothing being appropriate and functional. Tailor the following guidelines to your own personal preferences and work situation.

A business woman's wardrobe should, at the very least, consist of the following clothing: a coat (in a solid color without trimming), a jacket, two sweaters, a daytime dress with simple lines, a business suit, two blazers, two skirts, two pairs of slacks, three blouses, and an evening dress. Select clothing styles that can be altered completely with accessory changes.

It will save you a lot of money if you commit to one dominant color and build your wardrobe around it. Choose from violet-blue, navy, dark green, tan, brown, gray or black. Color variety can be introduced in less expensive accessories. The more expensive clothing items—such as a coat, a suit or a dress—should be purchased first because they will serve as the basis for all of your other wardrobe items.

Sheer, see-through clothing, low-cut necklines or frilly designs are not functional in a business setting and are not considered appropriate professional wear.

Accessories

One garment with different accessories can look like three different outfits. Pick accessories that will improve, not confuse the natural lines of your clothing.

Shoes

Quality shoes are a better investment from both an aesthetic and a functional point of view. Footwear for work should have built-in, cushioned support systems that offer comfort. Styles should be plain, such as low-heeled walking pumps made of patent leather, leather or suede. You will need different shades in brown, navy blue and black. To prevent leather shoes from cracking, waterproof them with silicone water repellent. If you keep your shoes on shoe trees, they will retain their shape much longer.

Purses

Purses can be relatively large but should never be out of proportion to your size. Invest in a quality attaché case; it is a must for the professional woman. When not in use, purses should be stuffed with wrapping tissue so that they will retain their shape.

Scarves

A scarf is the most versatile accessory that you can have in your wardrobe. Scarves will give your office attire a more polished effect. They come in a variety of finishes, shapes, colors and sizes. You can modify the appearance of a long neck by wearing a scarf across your neck and shoulders. If your neck is short, create the illusion of length by wearing an oblong scarf to draw the eyes down.

There are three different types of scarf clips. The type you need will depend upon the size and the weight of the material from which the scarf is made. A clip with a small loop is good for lightweight or narrow scarves; a medium loop is for larger scarves of heavier fabric; a large loop is for yet larger scarves made from the thickest fabric.

Many department stores offer classes on scarf tying. Check with one of the stores in your area and arrange an appointment with one of their qualified scarf consultants. If you can not find someone locally, you can write for information on Lorriane Hammett's books, *Living With Scarves* and *The Knaughty Look*. Mail queries to: Hammett Enterprises, 5250 Finch Ave. E., Unit 6, Scarborough, Ontario, Canada M1S 5A4.

Jewelry

The size of your jewelry pieces should be in proportion to your overall frame. If you are small-boned, for example, large, chunky jewelry will overpower you; if you are tall and full-figured, small pieces will look undersized. Inexpensive pieces, if chosen with care, can look more costly than their actual value. Pearl earrings and a string of pearls are always a good investment. As for gold jewelry, it is considered more dressy than silver. Polished stones, mounted in poorly finished settings, can look garish and are considered poor taste.

When purchasing a necklace, consider the contours of your face. If your face is thin and your neck long, you will want to create the illusion of width by wearing shorter strands. If your face is round and full, your objective will be to select longer necklaces to create the illusion of length. When you want to slenderize the look of your face, select stones or beads that are irregularly shaped. If your face is thin, oval or round stones and beads will soften angular features.

Always coordinate your earrings to match your necklace or pin. They do not have to match exactly but they should resemble the same basic decorative style. Do not let the size of your earrings over-power the size of your earlobes.

Avoid wearing gaudy jewelry, dangling earrings or jangling bracelets during office hours. This type of jewelry is too conspicuous for the business professional. Observe other stylish business women to see how they use accessories.

Considerations in Selecting Eyewear

Properly fitted eyeglasses are, of course, essential. Eyewear should fit securely and be able to stay in place without fussing. When selecting eyewear, you will also want to consider the following factors: the size and shape of your face, your facial features, your natural coloring, the color and design of the frames, the color of the lenses, the application of your eye makeup. If you have trouble trying to select the right eyewear, consult an optician.

Suggestions on Makeup for Eyeglass Wearers

The style of your specific eyewear, frames and lenses will determine how you should apply your eye cosmetics. If you are nearsighted you will want to make your eyes appear larger. On the other hand, lenses that correct farsightedness will magnify the appearance of eyes. If you are farsighted, apply eye makeup sparingly.

Darker frames require stronger cheek and lipstick shades to balance color. Cheek color should never be applied to the point where it disappears under eyeglass frames.

Do Your Fashion Homework

Add a "Current Fashion" file to your New Image Workbook by clipping out pictures of dressing ideas. Then, look through it when you want to re-accessorize an outfit. Experiment ahead of time with different clothing combinations. You will be surprised at how many varied looks you can create when you're not pressed for time. Be sure to jot down these different combinations on a note pad so that you can refer to these looks later.

Colors That Compliment You

Each of us has our own unique coloration. A combination of skin, eye and hair colors establishes the color schemes that will work best for us. Wearing the appropriate colors will enhance your overall appearance, produce dramatic effects and inspire compliments. Conversely, wearing unflattering shades will drain your complexion of vitality and make you appear to be tired.

There are many self-proclaimed color experts. However, only a wardrobe consultant (with an extensive background in color) has the expertise to assist you in determining the precise color combinations that will do the most for you. Remember that there is no substitute for going to a professional color expert. If your budget won't permit a visit, you can still make a study of color on your own. The next best thing to having a color consultation is having a good color reference book written by a color expert. A selected list of books written by color specialists can be found at the end of the book in the Recommended Reading for this chapter.

Psychological Effects of Color

Research has proven that color has a powerful effect upon the subconscious. The results of major personality studies, like the Rorschach test—in which the reactions of thousands of patients were recorded, compared, and analyzed—reveal that color responses are tied more to human emotions than to intellect. In her book, *The Psychology of Color and Design*, Dr. Deborah Sharpe investigates the effects of color and establishes its utilization in personal living and in the business and industrial worlds. According to Dr. Sharpe's studies, people attach all kinds of different meanings to color. Some of the associations she cites in her book are: red is believed to convey energy, heat, and noise; brown is cited as rich and healthy; purple is represented as a color of dignity and majesty; orange is perceived as bright and active.

Making Color Work For You

Color conveys many unspoken messages. Since it can be used as a method of subtle persuasion, it would be wise to learn more about the psychology of color and color symbolism in order to grasp its significance. Understanding color phenomena could be of vital importance to your major business encounters. Furthermore, it could assist you in exercising control over the emotional effect which certain colors inspire.

Color is associated with personal characteristics and can be perceived by others as an outer expression of your inner emotions. Therefore, the colors that you wear should always feel right to you.

Never surround yourself with colors that you are indifferent to or that conflict with your personality. Remember that color reaches the human subconscious and has the power to make a statement of its own. In his book, *The Luscher Color Test Book*, Dr. Max Luscher offers you an opportunity to find out just how psychologically revealing your color choices can be. The principle behind the Luscher Color Test is that accurate psychological information can be gained about a person through his or her choices and rejections of various colors.

Wardrobe Consultants

In the motion picture industry, the complicated task of insuring that clothes complement the actor's role is handled by professional designers. It is their job to make sure that the wardrobe projects the correct image. If you doubt that you are capable of assembling an image that makes you look as good as you are, then you may want to seriously consider hiring a professional with a critical eye to assist you. A wardrobe consultant can design an individualized, long-range wardrobe plan, coordinate your entire wardrobe, suggest the right accessories, recommend the necessary alterations and offer guidance on shopping.

Beauty of Aging

One of the factors that will have a profound effect upon your appearance is age. Aging is a natural process of life that comes with the advancement of years. The physical changes that occur as a result of aging slowly strip away the signs of youth. It makes no sense to live in fear of these changes; they will eventually happen to everyone.

Every woman who reaches middle age experiences some uneasiness about getting older. Those who have the hardest time coping are women who are the most reluctant to face it. Each gray hair, each additional pound and each crow's foot throw them into a frenzy. One of the quickest ways that a woman can add years to her appearance is in trying to look young by force. By denying the aging process, or by constantly trying to pass as younger, women unnecessarily torment themselves. Although there is nothing wrong with looking younger than one's years, it is extreme and irrational to constantly focus on it to the degree that it becomes an obsession. It is truly remarkable just how many women in this country are brainwashed into thinking that every wrinkle is a catastrophe.

Most of the distress over aging comes from living in a youth orientated culture. After all, this is a society where aging women are viewed in harsher terms than aging men. In their book, *Beyond The Male Myth*, Anthony Pietropinto, M.D., and Jacqueline Simenauer write, "Youth has never been particularly valued in men, not because it is unattractive, but because the years invariably allow men to acquire more desirable attributes." In other words, men become more distinguished with age ... and women become haggard.

The social stigma about aging will change only when women change their outlook and become less threatened by the idea of getting older. Women need to recondition their thinking by acquiring a positive philosophy about the passage of time. The success of aging requires both an internal and an external effort. Strong-minded, intellectually self-contained women recognize that aging can not be left to chance. Instead, it requires a strategy that involves these women in a new way of thinking and seeing themselves as they grow older. In his book, *It Takes A Long Time To Become Young*, Garson Kanin writes, "We ought to accept the fact that each decade of one's life, indeed each year, has its own colors and qualities, its strengths and weaknesses."

The potential rewards of aging are many. With the transition of years, women gain not just wrinkles but experience, wisdom and insight. They acquire sophistication, empowerment and autonomy, and their roles proliferate. There is more to beauty than the physical manifestation of youth. There is no reason why a woman's later years in life can not be her best years.

Merits Of Middle Age

Keeping a positive frame of mind about yourself will help you to combat any fears or doubts you may hold about the aging process. The key to aging successfully is to belong to your age and to celebrate it. Make yourself look as pleasing as possible and, in doing so, you will free your mind for more productive pursuits. Maintain your independence, moderate your habits and keep active.

Once, when asked about growing older, Chief Justice Earl Warren replied, "I'm very pleased with each advancing year. It stems back to when I was forty. I was a bit upset about reaching that milestone, but an older friend consoled me, 'Don't complain about getting old. Many, many people do not have that privilege.'"

Aging Characteristics

Thinking about aging is what makes you age. Regardless of how old you actually are, the following traits will make you feel and appear older: sarcasm … skepticism … boredom … dwelling on the past … preoccupation with aches and pains … vanity … arrogance … laziness and inactivity … inattention to others … self-pity.

Ageless Qualities

Your beauty will flourish at any age if you retain the following ageless qualities: passionate disposition … sensuality … positive mental attitude … sense of humor … lively curiosity about life … sense of adventure … a genuine interest in others … willingness to learn new things … vitality … easygoing nature … sense of purpose and involvement … inner satisfaction.

Setting Goals that Can Change Your Life

*E*verything we are now experiencing in the real world started out as just an imaginary thought. Shaped by our thinking, both consciously and unconsciously, our life as we know it is just a product of our mental picturing. We need to believe in the power of our own imagination. As children we were told that day dreaming was a waste of time. Nothing could be further from the truth. Imagine if Geraldine Ferraro would not have envisioned that she could be the first woman to run for election to high office on a major party ticket. Or, if Clara Barton had not imagined herself establishing the American Red Cross. And, where would Estee Lauder (the woman whose name is synonymous with the art of feminine beauty) be if she had not dared to dream that she could change the face of the cosmetics' industry forever. These three successful women all have one thing in common: they accomplished what they set out to do.

If we are dissatisfied with our lives we can transform them by defining what it is we really want ... and by making a commitment to obtain it. You can have what you want! A much better, happier, more financially rewarding life is within reach. We are always free to choose a different future. Whatever we direct our attention toward, we create. Our goals determine whether we prosper happily, or suffer frustration and loss. In this chapter, we'll discuss how to manage and direct your life ... to get what you really want.

We are all, to a certain extent, skilled at keeping joy out of our lives. Many people deny their physical, emotional, and spiritual needs. When a certain desire arises, a voice inside them says they shouldn't have that feeling, and they extinguish it. Our inner desires can be suppressed for years, until we no longer believe they are possible, or that we have the right to have them met.

Think about all the unfulfilled dreams you still have. Is there some place you have always wanted to visit, or something special you have always wanted to do? Maybe you would like to go back to school, buy a house, take a cruise, learn a foreign language, write music, or start your own business. The possibilities are endless. Isn't it time to reassess your priorities and start doing some of the things that will bring you true happiness? The question you need to ask yourself is, "How much joy in life am I willing to allow myself?"

Many of the limitations in our lives are self-imposed. Just assume for a moment that someone was to offer you a magic formula that would absolutely guarantee that you could satisfy your needs and achieve your innermost desires. What would you be willing to compromise to get your hands on such priceless information? Undoubtedly, you would be willing to forfeit quite a lot. But do you know that the magic formula is nothing more than mere goal setting? Goals provide a way by which any dream within reason may be attained. Fortune favors the person who is willing to make the effort to write out their great ideas and set a time limit on obtaining them.

Where we find ourselves today is the result of the actions we took yesterday. If we feel deprived and lack many of the things that make life worth living, maybe it is because we have failed to take the initiative to bring more pleasure into our day-to-day lives. Perhaps in the past we tried to introduce some change into our humdrum routine, but we neglected to write out our goals and direct our actions and subsequently, our efforts were thwarted.

Imagine what it would be like to embark on a long journey without planning ahead. It would be impossible to reach your final destination without a compass or a map, aiding you in navigating your course. You would have no way of knowing if you were going in the right direction or if you took a wrong turn. Such a trip would result in pandemonium. Goals help us organize and direct ourselves. They guard us against destructive habits of procrastination, inattention and negligence.

Be Passionate About Your Goals

No matter what goals you choose, they must be worth the work. The reason for this is simple: without passion, we cannot reasonably expect ourselves to work effectively and productively. Motivation *matters*. There will be hard times when all you will have is your dreams to sustain you. The most important thing to remember is that nothing worthwhile comes easily. If it did, it would not be that desirable because it would lack the thrill of accomplishment through personal effort.

Making Your Dreams Come True

Put your imagination to work and let it create what you want. See yourself as if you have already accomplished your goal. Many athletes use this successful technique before major sporting events. Celebrities in the world of entertainment, politics, and business have all relied on visualization to help guarantee positive outcomes.

To visualize, you must sit quietly with your eyes closed. Get a clear picture of exactly what you want to achieve in your mind. Pretend you are the director of your own documentary. Give yourself the starring role. Envision as many details as you can, and enlist as many of your physical senses as possible. Remember, the unconscious has no power to grasp abstract ideas, so you must present it with a vivid picture. Actually see yourself achieving your desire. Get excited! You will be delighted with the potent feeling of success that fills you. Give your goals strength and vitality by dwelling upon them. Spend a few minutes a day practicing mental imagery and you will increase your probability of success.

It is also a good idea to mount colorful photographic images of your goal on a large poster board. Place the board in a location where you can glance at it every day. By doing this, you will impress these images on your subconscious mind.

Affirmations

Another way to reinforce your goals is to make up affirmations that you faithfully recite on a daily basis. Affirmations are positive statements—no more than one or two sentences—that you repeat to yourself at intervals during the day to strengthen your purpose, reassure you and inflate your confidence. These useful phrases can be used as a form of self-talk to counterattack any underlying negative thoughts that might prevent you from believing that you can actually accomplish your goal. When a destructive emotion strikes you, you can use affirmations to neutralize your mind. If practiced regularly, in time your affirmations will embed themselves in your unconscious mind and you will accept them as fact. Keep a piece of paper in your pocket with your affirmations on it, and carry it with you at all times. Repeat your affirmations out loud throughout the day.

Consider the possibility of recording your affirmations onto a blank cassette. This would give you an opportunity to listen to the tape while putting on your makeup, commuting to and from work, doing chores around the house or while exercising.

Create Your Own Circle of Backers and Supporters

As you start to accomplish your goal, some of the people you are closest to may feel threatened or try to compete with you. Be prepared for it. Watch out for sabotage from associates, friends, family members, children, or your spouse. In many cases, you will have to just grin-and-bear it, but you can still limit your exposure to those who do not believe in your abilities or who criticize your actions constantly. Surround yourself, instead, with people who want to see you accomplish your goal. Few of us succeed without allies. Be selective. It is far better to cultivate an association with one person who honors you than three who do not.

Take time to develop rewarding relationships with individuals who have a genuine desire to help you. Do not be afraid to ask for their guidance when necessary. They can expand your way of thinking by offering you intelligent solutions to problems and by alerting you to possible opportunities that you might have otherwise overlooked.

Commit to a Completion Time

In order to achieve our goals, we must not only plan for them, but be prepared to set a time frame for their completion. Goals can only be accomplished through action, not through endless planning to take action. It is, therefore, of the utmost importance to commit to a date of completion. You have 10,080 minutes, or 168 hours, every week (depending on how you see it) to work toward your goal. Budget your time wisely. Many of the most effective tasks take no more than a moment or two to complete.

You will never achieve your desire if you grope aimlessly for it. You must approach your goal directly. Once you have established what you want, set your target, plan and proceed in a practical manner. Collect all data related to your goal, do research, compile information and study it. Books, magazines, trade journals, and private consultants will also provide you with practical advice. You can reach your goal if you steadfastly follow through to successful completion.

Organize Yourself

Do you find yourself saying, "I never have enough time for anyone or anything," even though you are not accomplishing very much with your time? That's not surprising. Few of us give conscious consideration to the expenditure of our time until we realize the precious and elusive nature of it. Time is much too valuable to waste. Organization is a major time-saver. The more organized you are, the more free time you will have at your disposal.

Lack of organization is a self-blocking technique that hinders you from having the time to work on your objectives. It is impossible to have order and clarity in your life when there is chaos. Confusion creates serious tension and prevents you from accomplishing the important goals you set for yourself.

Disorder is inconvenient and time-consuming. If you waste your money you can always earn more, but if you waste your time, no amount of money can buy it back. Concentrate on how you can become more efficient. Organizing yourself might include anything from revising your time schedule (getting up earlier to accomplish more, for example) to simplifying some of your daily rituals, such as sorting out closets, cabinets and drawers. The following timesaving measures and organizing techniques will assist you in the process of establishing order.

☐ Purchase a compact notebook and calendar you can carry with you. Write in it things you want to accomplish, errands you need to run, impending appointments and any other information you will need to keep close at hand.

☐ One of the quickest ways to become frazzled and loose track of precious time is to spend it trying to locate things when you're in a hurry. Consider placing the objects you use the most in more practical locations.

☐ Look around your home and your work space and spot problem areas that need to be reworked to function more efficiently. Revise any system that is not working well for you.

☐ Set up an inventory control system for household items and check it regularly. When you are running low on something, add it to a list of replacement supplies.

There are many books and audio cassettes on the subject of time management. See the Recommended Reading section at the end of the book.

Analyze Yourself With Ruthless Honesty

The image we have of ourselves determines how far we go in life. High self-esteem is essential to success. Simply stated, we are who we think we are. We can actually predict what our future will be depending on our sense of self-worth. People that lack self-confidence have many hidden fears that plague them and hold them back. They constantly sabotage their efforts to get ahead because they secretly feel they don't deserve anything better. In order for you to obtain your goals, you must be willing to accept what you desire and know in your heart that you deserve to have it.

Make a careful study of yourself. Unhappy experiences and defeats have power. Empty your mind of your past mistakes and failures. Remember, each new day gives you another chance. Start appreciating yourself. Give yourself credit for who and what you are. You are a very special human being who is capable of creating anything you choose, provided you believe in yourself and your abilities.

Take a moment right now to make an accurate self-assessment of your strengths and weaknesses, and honor yourself accordingly. Write down in detail what makes you a valuable person. Always recognize your worth and respect your abilities. Do not demand too much or too little of yourself. Only *you* know what your potential is and what your true limitations are. When you feel good about yourself, you radiate confidence and others feel good about you, too.

Free Yourself from What You Don't Want

Before you can determine what your future goals will be, you must first make a list of what you want to eliminate from your life. This is vital because it is impossible to pour fresh, new ideas into a mind that is already corrupted with an accumulation of miscellaneous thoughts. We can get so wrapped up in problems of the past and present that we have no time left to plan for better things. Every new stage of life requires renunciation. Every growth and gain means the rejection of something old. Therefore, cleansing is the first step to goal setting.

To perform this exercise, you will need to schedule some uninterrupted time for yourself, at least twenty minutes. Put on some tranquil music. Get comfortable. Now take a piece of paper and draw a line down the middle. On the left side of the paper, list all the things about your life you dislike. Be sure to mention all the things, conditions, and people you want to eliminate from your life. On the right side, list all the aspects of your life that you are perfectly happy and content with, and do not wish to change. This process will assist you in freeing up your mind and preparing you for the positive things you want to create in your life.

You now have the choice of going even further and disposing of any material possessions that no longer hold any value for you. This is of the utmost importance because it helps you make way for your true desires. By letting go of these things, you release vast reservoirs of wealth. When you cling to objects that you have no further use for, you are demonstrating fearfulness, not expectancy. Hoarding objects keeps them from others who might benefit from them. Give these things to family members, friends or to charity and experience a magnificent lightness within you.

Creating Your Life As You Want It

Now that you have gone though the elimination and cleansing process, you should be ready to write out your goals. Begin by dividing your desires into the following three sections:

Personal development goals. Who do you want to be intellectually, spiritually, physically?

Material goals. What things do you want to acquire? A new car, new home, a new wardrobe, something else?

Economic goals. How much money do you want to make in one year, three years, five years, ten years, twenty years?

Let your mind wander. Give no thought to what others insist is important for your happiness. Only write down what *you* feel will bring you maximum fulfillment. The bottom line is that our desires can only come from deep inside us. No one else can make these choices for us.

Do not restrict your desires. Be childlike. Children have the capacity to believe their fantasies are possible. The child inside us is ageless. Tell yourself you can have anything you want. Just write down your desires. Allow five minutes for each section. Write as fast as you can. Be specific so you do not end up with something you don't want.

You should now have an idea of the things you most want to bring into your life. Examine your three lists carefully. Go back and circle three top desires for each category. On a separate sheet of paper for each division, list the goal. Next to it write down the time you intend to complete this goal. Be specific. Place a number next to it to indicate one, three, five, ten or twenty years. Now write out the benefits in reaching that goal. Below the benefits, write out the major obstacles you will have to overcome to accomplish the goal. Next, write out the skills, or the knowledge, that will be required to obtain it. Lastly, list the names of individuals, groups and organizations to work with that may be able to assist you in accomplishing this goal.

Congratulations! You now have a plan of action. You will reach your goals if you are ambitious, willing to work hard, willing to take the risks involved and accept the changes you must make to accommodate your desires. Keep in mind that no goal is engraved in stone. Feel free to change your goals as your life unfolds. If your desires are only surface desires, they will pass away. But if your desires are deep-seated, they will remain with you until you have accomplished them.

An important feature of goal setting is that it provides you with a tangible, permanent record of what you really what. You cannot lose by writing out your goals. The only way you'll fail is when you stop writing them out. Always have a definite goal in mind and write it down. Never let yourself drift or you will become a victim of circumstances. Writing your goals down will help you to visualize your desires and to decide what changes you want to make in the immediate and distant future. Whether you produce changes or not depends upon how honest you are about what you really want … and how much you are willing to do to get it.

Make a Success Notebook for the Future

Nothing succeeds like success. Celebrate the thrill of both major and minor triumphs. When you achieve a goal, be sure to document it in a success notebook. Goals need not be significant; they can even be inconsequential. But, log your accomplishments. In doing so, you will feel as if you have advanced even after overcoming the smallest of obstacles. We often do far more than we set out to do.

Dreams don't just come true; we make them come true. Give yourself credit for your accomplishments. By writing out your list of achievements, you come to value who you are and whom you are becoming. There will be rough periods in your life when your success notebook will bring you much comfort. It will serve as a reminder to you of what you are capable of and will help you to stay centered in times of disillusionment. As you work toward your dream, minor problems and disappointments are inevitable. Having a written record of your own competence will make small setbacks easier to take. When a goal is completed, there is a feeling of gratification that lasts a long time.

Acquire the habit of writing out exactly how you accomplished your victories. You only have so much time and so much energy, so make notes on what worked and what didn't. As one goal is achieved, another is chosen. In the years to come, you will be able to utilize this information when you're trying to reach other goals.

Continue to Set Goals for Yourself

Setting and striving for goals help us to maintain an enthusiasm about life. To keep ahead of our accomplishments, we must move on to more lofty aspirations to satisfy our future desires. After you have attained an objective, set a new one, again with a time limit. Keep up this progressive series of goals for yourself. Make goal setting a regular habit; the very act of goal setting clears your mind and focuses your life. It forces you to dream in specifics, not generalities. Once a person has gone through the goal setting process, creative breakthroughs begin to occur. When you know what you want, you begin to attract to yourself the ideas, opportunities, people and events that are necessary to make your dream a reality.

Goal Action Plan

List Only Goals You Can Work On Each Day

Goal Action Plan for _____
                                    NAME   DATE

Step #1   Identify Your Goal _____

_____

_____

Completion Date: _____

Step #2   Benefits of Reaching this Goal _____

_____

_____

Step # 3   Major Obstacles to Overcome in Reaching this Goal _____

_____

_____

Step #4   Skills or Knowledge Required to Reach This Goal _____

_____

_____

Step #5   Individuals, Groups and Organizations to Work with

in Reaching This Goal _____

_____

_____

Step #6   Plan Of Action to Reach this Goal _____

_____

_____

_____

CHAPTER 12

The Power of Negotiation

*W*omen who know how to bargain for what they want have a stronger sense of control over their lives. Women who don't feel helpless and insecure the minute they encounter a confrontation. If women want to resolve their difficulties and not be victimized by others, they need to learn how to negotiate properly.

To achieve and hold positions of power we must be able to use information to affect the behavior of others we come in contact with. Most women have difficulty negotiating, not because they lack intelligence or ability, but because they have never been taught the basic principles. This chapter is designed to help you reach your objectives when negotiating.

Practically everything in life involves negotiation. For instance, when we rent, buy or sell something, or introduce an idea, we negotiate. Whenever we have a dispute of any kind and we enter into a discussion to settle it, we are negotiating. The art of negotiation is learned. There is no such thing as a born negotiator, although some people are better at it than others. Charismatic individuals can temporarily sway people, but the potential for a misunderstanding later on is almost inevitable. If we want results from our interactions with others, we must be prepared to communicate our position in an intelligently persuasive manner. Charm is no substitute for a knowledgeable approach to successful bargaining.

Formulate Your Plan for Discussion Beforehand

The first principle of successful negotiation is to be prepared in advance. Never go into negotiation without knowing what you want the outcome to be. Having an agenda for discussion will set the tempo for what follows.

Putting together an agenda requires careful planning. An agenda can disclose or conceal motives. Know what your real needs are, your priorities, and what your deadline is. Ask yourself, "What is the worst that can happen if we cannot reach an agreement?" Be sure that you have a definite alternative if you cannot reach a settlement. The person who will benefit the most from any negotiation is the one with the best alternative. They always end up the winner.

Take the time to decide beforehand how issues can best be introduced. Whenever possible, devise a number of solutions that the person you're negotiating with can choose from. You will have to include reasons and motivation if you expect your suggestions to be taken seriously. Be aware of your strong points and how to make the best use of them. If you need to acquire additional knowledge from an outside party, or an expert, do not fail to do so. Don't wait until the last moment to coordinate all the details. It will be well worth your while to have your strategy together before that first meeting. Don't expect to fake it. If you haven't done your homework, the other party will know it. Give a great deal of consideration to your closing remarks. Summarize your main points and ask yourself, "What thought do I most want my opponent to walk away with at the end of the discussion?"

Rehearse Your Agenda First

Once you have established your agenda, ask a friend, family member or close associate to listen to your proposal and play the role of "devil's advocate." Request that they address hard-line questions to you. Your best defense is to answer these types of questions ahead of time. The more time you have to think about what you will be asked, the better your answers will be.

Always Investigate

Before negotiating, think about the person with whom you will be dealing. Try to learn as much as you can about your opponent's point of view in advance. Never assume anything. Assumptions can be deceiving, although you must make assumptions about the opposing party. The important thing to remember is that they are, at best, only uneducated guesses. Make an effort to prove them right or wrong as soon as possible. Learn as much as you can about the history of the person with whom you will be negotiating. Become as familiar with their organizational structure as possible.

Most importantly, find out the limits of their authority. If their superiors have final authority over their decisions, investigate to firmly establish who's approval will be necessary to consummate the deal. Never negotiate with anyone who has no decision-making authority. Be prepared to walk out if, at the last minute, the authority changes. One of the reasons it is so important to understand the authority structure before you negotiate is to avoid becoming the victim of the missing person tactic.

The Missing Person Tactic

A frequent tactic used in negotiation is to defer a final decision to an absent authority figure. In this maneuver, you are confronted during the final phase of negotiations with the convenient absence of the person with the final authority. This is a common tactic that is frequently used to delay the final agreement. If used on you, this tactic can benefit the person you're negotiating with and hamper your negotiations in any of the following ways:

☐ The other party has the option of deferring to obtain more information or can close the deal when convenient to them.

☐ It can be used as a method to temper your aspirations by preventing you from making larger demands.

☐ The other party can negotiate elsewhere, using your agenda as a starting point.

☐ The person you're negotiating with can permanently break off talks and retreat if they feel it is necessary.

In some cases, at the last moment, the missing person may reappear and demand further concessions. This, of course, would naturally weaken your bargaining position; you just might consider conceding more points rather than risk loosing the deal entirely.

What Your Opponent Wants From You

The other party wants many of the same things you want: to be listened to, to be acknowledged, to establish a sense of truth and to be able to count on your integrity. The person you're negotiating with will also want to know that you are making a sincere effort to extend yourself to him or her. What your opposition does not want is to be unfairly manipulated and to deal with surprises and last minute changes that drag the negotiations on endlessly.

Bargaining is always a risk. There's no doubt about it. Each of the parties involved has self-esteem at stake and that can be intimidating. People get anxious when they are vulnerable. Be thoughtful and make an effort to do what you can to put yourself and your negotiating partner at ease.

Starting The Negotiation

Your approach at the onset of the negotiation is of utmost importance. Be mindful of the attitude you convey. Never appear stressed in front of the other party. Speak in a well-modulated and deliberate voice. Show that you are mentally alert, poised, and confident by the way you walk, sit and stand. The tone of your voice, your facial expressions, and your posture will greatly affect the initial response you get from the other side.

Address the other party with tact and respect for their dignity. Show a concern for their needs and feelings. It is a whole different world when you see it through your negotiating partner's eyes. Begin on a positive note by immediately establishing what you both have in common. Employ friendly small talk and chat briefly about the situation, the weather, or the daily news. Establish mutual interests in your warm up comments. These mutual interests can be the basis for friendly communications in the future.

Study Your Opponent

You can tell a lot about a person by the way they orally express themselves. Listening is a skill that improves with practice. Hear what your opponent is really saying by isolating the key words and phrases he or she uses. Pay special attention to the person's mood. The way in which the other party phrases their sentences will indicate their emotional temperature at the moment. Weigh their words carefully to determine if they are excited, angry, indifferent to what you are saying, or are trying to impress you. Obtain as much information as possible about the other person's value system, prejudices, likes and dislikes. Most importantly, establish where you both agree...and where you disagree. Never interrupt or contradict your opponent while he or she is talking.

Be careful not to make gestures that indicate you agree with what is being said unless that is the case. Smiling and nodding conveys understanding and could be misconstrued. Make an effort to subvert the natural inclination we all have to be agreeable with our body language.

Evaluate the Other Party's Body Language

Identifying your opponent's body language is another way to determine his or her state of mind. If the other party is leaning forward toward you, there is a good chance he or she is attentive and is taking in the information. If the other person is holding back his or her shoulders, even slightly, it may indicate that he or she is distracted and is withdrawing from the conversation. Rapid, exaggerated, or abrupt movements could be interpreted as impatience or intolerance on their part.

Another important clue to a person's attitude is eye contact. Observe the other person to determine if their eyes are focused on you, or if they are wandering, and thus avoiding eye contact.

When dealing with your opposition you must remain attentive. The message here is a simple one. Keep your eyes and ears open at all times. Be particularly aware of the way your opponent's body is positioned during your conversation. A person with rigid posture is less flexible and will probably offer more resistance to your suggestions.

Every Negotiation Is Loaded With Possibilities

Start off by discussing uncomplicated issues, and then gradually work your way up to more controversial matters. Be careful not to exasperate your opponent by overwhelming them with too many ideas, at least initially. State your case moderately; it will disarm your opponent and minimize any friction that may exist.

Let the other side know that you are entering into the negotiation process determined to reach a mutually acceptable solution. If you use this positive approach, you will most likely gain their support. The solution to a situation most often lies in the combined mental efforts of both you and the other party. As you move through the negotiation process, keep an open mind. Treat ideas with respect; each one is worthy of consideration.

How To Handle a Difficult Person

Sometimes, no matter how congenial you are, you may still encounter hostility from the "opposition." Don't allow negative emotions to surface. Doubt, fear, anger and rage will interfere with your good judgment. Whatever the provocation, remember it is counter-productive to give in to arguments. Flare-ups break down communications and ruin pending deals. When a destructive feeling strikes you, neutralize it by focusing on what the real issues are and your ultimate objective.

Regardless of how obnoxious you may think the other party is, never be abrasive. Stay centered and express yourself clearly and decisively. Desperate and irrational behavior on the part of your opponent will more than likely result in their eventual embarrassment. If you remain calm, it will work to your advantage. The more confident you are, the less you have to do to prove your point. Think twice before you lose your temper; it is a sure sign of weakness. Be as pleasant as you can be, and as unpleasant as you have to be. But, whatever you do or say, take care not intimidate, threaten, accuse or humiliate the other party. Be direct but non-confrontational.

Timing Is Everything

Trying to rush negotiations inevitably puts one party in jeopardy. Always allow for acknowledgment time. Your patience will ultimately pay off. Transactions start with all kinds of false assumptions and misconceptions. Both parties enter into negotiations assuming that their unrealistic goals will be easily met. The process of bargaining generally takes both parties by surprise. Each party is forced to re-evaluate their priorities. People require time to reconcile their original expectations with the reality of more tempered negotiating aims. Every negotiation deserves an acceptance phase: a time for both parties to adjust and to mentally prepare for compromise.

Addressing the Other Party's Concerns

Never answer a question until you are sure of what is being asked. Don't feel you must answer every question that is directed to you. Some questions will not merit an immediate response. There may be questions that you will wish to delay answering until you have more complete knowledge. Ask for more time to explore the issue and prepare an appropriate response. Know in advance what you do not want to reveal. Don't be annoyed if the other party interrupts you. Allow them to; their reply can be enlightening.

Study and Evaluate the Other Party's Plan

Never accept the other party's agenda without thinking about it first. Go over their suggested plan to evaluate what it does not include. Be skeptical of getting too good a deal. Carefully consider all the advantages and disadvantages that come to mind. If you have objections and do not like what is being presented, speak out. Make sure your viewpoint is understood as soon as possible. Failure to do so could complicate talks and delay a settlement. Objections are always raised during negotiations; it is best to handle them the moment they arise rather than bring them up later when they are more difficult to deal with.

Making Concessions

Concessions have a way of shifting the balance of power; they should be made to bring you closer to your goal. They can provide you with leverage if you keep track of how many you have made.

Never make a concession until you know all the demands. Know yourself well enough to understand what concessions you can live with. Whatever you claim you are going to give up, you should be prepared to actually relinquish it. Don't be too eager to make the first concession on an important issue. The other party will put a greater value on the things that are harder to get.

You do not have to match what the other party gives up. Nor are they obligated to match your concessions. Although you and your opponent may both wish to be reasonable, you are bound to have difficulty doing so. Always keep in mind that an eventual settlement is more important than individual issues.

Once the other party has agreed to a concession, do not comment on the logic of his or her decision—it may be misinterpreted. Such a statement during this critical period could upset the other party and put you in an awkward position; focus on your next strategic move instead.

Negotiating by Telephone

During the negotiation process, an unexpected telephone call from the other party could be a premeditated tactic. The person making the call might be attempting to gain the advantage after using some time to prepare. The person receiving the unanticipated call, however, is in a weaker bargaining position because they have had no time to plan for this unexpected telephone meeting.

If you are the recipient of such a sudden call, tell the person calling that you have pressing concerns that need to be addressed at the moment and cannot talk. Perhaps you have an appointment scheduled and are already late for it. Offer to get back to the caller at their convenience. This puts you in the position of caller, with equal time to prepare.

Prepare a checklist of the points you want to cover and gather together all your reference materials beforehand. Return the call from a place where you will not be distracted. At the end of your conversation, summarize what you agreed upon and what follow-up action will be taken.

If you need to leave a phone message, make sure that it is concise. Use a straightforward approach and stick to the point. If your message is lengthy, mention how many topics you will be covering at the beginning of the call. Never use a speaker phone unless you are on a conference call and you have warned the other party ahead of time. Unless otherwise specified, make sure you return all telephone calls within 24 hours. Under no circumstances leave a call unanswered. Take advantage of commonly used voice mail to leave concise and to-the-point messages that highlight your negotiating stance.

Get It in Writing

No agreement, no matter how carefully negotiated, is worth much unless it is in writing. Never assume an agreement or a sale has been made until the contract has been signed or money has exchanged hands. A promise is merely that...just a promise. It is also wise to remember that there are always loopholes in every contract. Be careful. Examine the agreement closely before you make that final handshake to close the deal.

How To Avoid Deadlock

In negotiations, a deadlock occurs when the overall differences between the two parties are too large to settle. Neither party in a negotiation benefits from deadlock. Never threaten to break off talks unless you have figured out a way to continue, even after you have given an ultimatum. In fact, try to refrain from giving absolute ultimatums if possible. On the other hand, if your opponent is pressuring you with the "last and final offer," don't be intimidated. There is a good chance he or she will probably be still willing to negotiate. It's best if you don't say or do anything in your frustration that will make it embarrassing for the other party to return to the negotiating table later on. Do not fall into a time deadline trap; many deadlines are negotiable.

Failing to Reach a Settlement

Nowhere is it written that all final agreements are fair and reasonable. There are going to be times when you cannot reach a full agreement. If this occurs, you may have to settle for a partial solution. In some instances it will be better than nothing. What is important in negotiating is that the parties involved achieve some level of satisfaction, at least enough to encourage them to sign an agreement.

We have all heard the expression, "You win some, you lose some." Sometimes we fail for reasons unrelated to our efforts, mainly because of circumstances that were out of our control. Few really great negotiators have flawless records. Remember, failure is a point of view, not a result. If you cannot arrive at a settlement, it does not mean you have to abandon hope for any future discussions. Times change. There still might be far more possibilities than you think. Someday, you may have another opportunity to renegotiate.

Create a Mistake File

Failure always teaches us. Your future strength as a negotiator or as a successful sales person will depend on how well you learn from your past mistakes. Write down in detail what you think were some of the common causes of your negotiating errors. Study them closely. This will keep you from repeating them over again. Be ready to apply this knowledge to your next bargaining session.

How to Negotiate a Sale

Everything we do in life is in some way related to selling. In fact, nothing happens until one person sells an idea, service or a piece of merchandise to another. Effective selling requires planning, preparation and practice.

To sell anything you must first present an idea, establish its truth and dismiss counter ideas. Most of us make the effort to obtain the necessary instruction on how to best present our product or service. We go through the trouble of furnishing our prospect with the adequate evidence to verify or back up our claims, but we do not devote the proper attention to eliminating counter ideas that are instinctively presented by the prospect as a barrier to the sale. More often than not, the prospect's objections are not the real obstacle in consummating the sale but are sign posts pointing to the prospect's real interests. If we were to pay attention to these objections, we would better understand the basis on which the sale could be made.

Handling Objections

Answering objections is one of the most important details involved in closing a sale. Generally, there are two phases of an objection that a prospect may present. The first is reluctance, which involves a series of excuses made by the prospect during the opening part of the sales presentation for the purpose of guarding his or her time. The second phase—the real objection—is given by the prospect after the sales presentation has been made.

The hesitations the prospect makes in the early stages of the sales presentation rarely account for anything, aside from the usual negative, habitual response. The prospect is merely safeguarding his or her time. The prospect may react by saying, "I have all the merchandise I need," "I can't afford it," or "I'm in a hurry." Each of these excuses means the same thing: lack of interest on the part of the prospect. You must be careful not to question these opening excuses; if confronted the prospect may become defensive. There is no sense in trying to convince your prospect that he or she can afford something that they do not want; this would be premature. Instead, shift the tone of the conversation to how your product or service can help the prospect solve a problem that you have been able to detect so far. As any good salesperson knows, "People do not buy goods and services, but rather, they buy solutions to their problems."

To get beyond the reluctance phase of the objection and begin to help the prospect identify his real needs, you must learn to become a creative problem solver. You cannot find a solution for your prospect's objections if you don't know what the problems are first. You will need to ask some questions ... and you will have to be prepared to listen carefully to the answers. With simple yet probing questions, try to find out a little about the prospect's business or if the prospect is currently using merchandise or services such as yours. Try to determine the prospect's wants and needs by asking open-ended questions that will help you gain valuable information, such as questions that begin with who, what, why, where and how.

No prospect will immediately accept your point of view. Telling your prospect that he or she has made the wrong decisions in the past about purchases or services—or commenting on his or her faults—will not endear you to them. The prospect's confidence is gained when you agree with the claims he or she is making about their specific problems. When you allow your prospect to express concerns, he begins to trust you. This is the time when you can begin to sway him to your way of thinking. To do this, you must first plant a seed in the prospect's mind on how your product or service will better relate to his or her particular needs.

When you speak, state only a few points at a time. If what you are trying to say becomes too cluttered with irrelevant remarks, you could end up boring or confusing the prospect. To emphasize your comments, use words that will paint vivid pictures in the prospect's mind. Avoid using technical terms when conversing with the prospect. Such terms are meaningless and will only complicate communication. Speak in your natural conversational manner and try to eliminate the clutter of "sales talk."

Objections generally are the result of ignorance or lack of complete understanding about the specific merchandise or service you are selling. For almost every objection based on misunderstanding, an appeasing response that will lead the prospect in the direction of the sale can be formulated, if you are willing to do a little planning in advance.

A true, positive mental attitude about your product or service offered goes a long way in persuading a prospective customer to do business with you. One thought must be paramount in your mind if you are going to be successful at securing the prospect's cooperation with the sale: "This prospect needs me." If you can be interested in your prospect and work hard at helping this individual to solve a problem or meet a need, that desire gets across to the prospect. On the other hand, if your mind is filled with thoughts of greed or sales to be made, those thoughts are also conveyed. Their confidence in you and their cooperation in helping you close the sale will vanish.

Encouraging Prospects to Make a Decision

Even if you are successful in convincing your prospect of the value of your product or service, they may procrastinate in making a decision. Few of us feel comfortable making decisions. Not only must you convince the prospect that you can provide them with the best solution to their problem, you must also create a sense of urgency to help them move swiftly through the decision making stage.

Availability, price and loss of opportunity are the three major reasons why people will make an immediate decision to buy. Focus on these three areas when you are giving your sales presentation and you will more than likely be successful in sales transactions.

Five Hot Tips on Selling

☐ Never keep a prospect waiting. Being late is disrespectful and tells the prospect where they stand on your list of priorities.

☐ Whenever possible, make an appointment with your prospect. Be thoughtful of the buyer's time restraints. Plan your presentation for the amount of time your prospect has available.

☐ Always strive to be professional, easy going, and informative. Do not try to pressure, harass or coerce people into making a decision against their will.

☐ Offer realistic projections of results and communicate clearly the limitations of your products and services.

☐ Leave yourself as much room as you can for negotiating by making your starting price as high as the competition will permit without overpricing your product or service. Setting upper-end price parameters allows the buyer to make an offer and enables them to negotiate for a better deal. Never promise a prospect what you cannot deliver.

Recommended Reading

Chapter One: **Coping with Stress**

14,000 Things To Be Happy About: The Happy Book by Barbara Ann Kipfer. Workman Publishing, New York, 1990. A quirky, irresistible list of the little things that make us happy: items, places, moods and thoughts.

You Can't Afford The Luxury Of A Negative Thought by John Roger and Peter McWilliams. Prelude Press, Los Angeles, 1991. This number one best seller is for people with any life-threatening illness, "including life" itself. It is full of humor and advice about overcoming negative thinking.

Living A Beautiful Life by Alexandra Stoddard. Avon Books, New York, 1986. This unique book offers hundreds of delightful suggestions on how to turn dull, irritating routines into life-enhancing rituals. It will help you to reduce stress, replenish your inner self and bring joy to every day of your life.

Living Through Personal Crisis by Ann Kaiser Sterns. Ballantine Books, New York, 1984. This book is about the small and large losses that occur in life. Kaiser-Sterns, a counselor for grieving persons, focuses on the lives of individuals who are struggling with depression and other symptoms of distress. Facing our losses is how we find our freedom again. That's how healing begins.

Treating Type A Behavior And Your Heart by Meyer Friedman, M.D. and Diane Ulmer, R.N., M.S. Alfred Knopf Publisher, New York, 1984. This book offers a new scope to treatment of persons at risk of having a heart attack. Type A behavior can be a significant factor in coronary heart disease. Freedman is convinced that Type As can modify their own behavior by changing their dangerous habit patterns. He outlines the specifics of a do-it-yourself program.

Stress Sanity and Survival by Robert L. Woolfolk, PH.D. and Frank C. Richardson, PH.D. Simon & Schuster, New York, 1978. This book goes far in putting the psychologist's insights, skills and tools into lay person's language. As a result, the reader can learn how to better cope with stress.

Stress Management: A Comprehensive Guide To Wellness by Edward Charlesworth, PH.D. and Ronald Nathan, PH.D. Ballantine/Self Help Publishers, New York, 1984. This easy to understand and follow guide identifies the specific areas of stress in life—family, work, social, emotional—and offers proven techniques for dealing with them. It also discusses the types of stress to reduce and the kinds of tension you can turn into positive motivation for your life.

AUDIO CASSETTES

Is It Worth Dying For? Dr. Robert Eliot. Bantam Audio Publishing, New York, 1987. This cassette is based on Dr. Eliot's book and offers suggestions on stress management.

When Am I Going To Be Happy? Penelope Russianoff, PH.D. Bantam Audio Publishing, New York, 1988. Dr. Russianoff, author of *Why Do I Think I'm Nothing Without A Man*, offers recommendations on how to break the emotional bad habits that keep you from reaching your potential happiness.

Chapter Two: Solving Everyday Problems

Choices: Making the Right Decisions in a Complex World by Lewis Lmedes. Harper & Row Publishers, San Francisco, 1986. Knowledge is power. You can apply the information in this book to change and enrich your life.

Overcoming Indecisiveness by Theodore Rubin, M.D. Harper & Row Publishers, New York, 1985. This book is all about understanding and solving problems. Rubin will be enormously helpful in assisting you in making decisions in all areas of your life.

Yes or No: The Guide to Better Decisions by Johnson Spencer, M.D. Harper Collins Publishers, New York, 1992. Johnson, co-author of *The One-Minute Manager*, presents a brilliant and practical system for making better decisions in your work and personal life.

Empowerment by David Gershon and Gail Straub. Delta Books, New York, 1989. This workbook is a powerful, practical and clear tool that will help heal and empower those attempting to face their problems.

AUDIO CASSETTES

How to Be Your Own Therapist by David Viscott. Audio Renaissance Tapes, Inc., Los Angeles, 1989. The ability to identify and solve problems is a skill that can be learned. Derived from one of his most popular seminars, Viscott assists in identifying deepest needs and helps you to obtain them.

Unconditional Life: Mastering the Forces that Shape Personal Reality by Deepak Chopra, M.D. Bantam Audio Publishing, New York, 1991. Chopra believes that to be totally free, we must first heal our emotions and our spirit. He offers techniques that will help master the forces necessary to achieve unlimited potential.

Chapter Three: Women in the Workplace

The Money Guide: How to Start and Run Your Business. To purchase a copy, write: Your Business, P.O. Box 30626, Tampa, FL 33630.

101 Practical Ways to Make Money At Home, by the editors of *Good Housekeeping Books,* New York.

Entrepreneur Magazine's Complete Guide to Owning a Home-Based Business, Bantam/Dell Publishers, New York, NY.

250 Home-Based Jobs: Innovative, Imaginative, Alternatives To The World Of 9-5 by Scott Olson. Arco Publishers, New York.

36 Small Business Mistakes and How To Avoid Them by Mark Stevens. Parker Publishing Co., West Nyack, New York.

The Success Syndrome: Hitting Bottom When You Reach The Top by Dr. Steven Berglas. Plenum Press, New York, 1986.

Beware The Naked Man Who Offers You His Shirt by Harvey MacKay. William Morrow Publishers, New York, 1990.

AUDIO CASSETTES

The Seven Habits Of Highly Effective People by Stephen Covey. Simon & Schuster Sound Ideas, New York, 1989.

Think And Grow Rich. Napoleon Hill. Success Motivation Cassettes, Waco, Texas.

The Entrepreneurial Life. David Silver. John Wiley & Sons, Inc., New York, 1986.

Swim With The Sharks Without Being Eaten Alive. Harvey Mackay. Sound Editions, Random House, New York, 1989.

Seasons Of Success. Dennis Waitley. Tapes include *How To Plan Your Success, How To Cultivate Your Success, How To Reap The Greatest Benefit From Your Success.* Tape Delta Media, Fullerton, Calif., 1986

The Secret To Staying Motivated. Zig Ziglar. Tape Delta Media, Fullerton, Calif.

Chapter Four: Being Single

Why Do I Think I Am Nothing Without A Man? by Penelope Russianoff, PH.D. Bantam Books, New York, 1981. Dr. Russianoff offers warm, straightforward and insightful advice on becoming sexually independent, becoming more supportive of yourself (emotionally and financially), learning to love being alone, and how a woman can be her own best friend.

Finding Love: Practical Advice For Men and Women by Sally Jesse Raphael. Arbor House, New York, 1984. Television and radio personality Sally Jesse Raphael offers sound advice on how to look for love, finding love the second time around, and dealing with the issues of age difference, money, occupation, children and lifestyle.

What Men Won't Tell You But Women Need To Know by Bob Berkowitz. William Morrow & Co., New York, 1990. There are thousands of unanswered questions about men that women have been forced to puzzle out for themselves, and more often than not, they have come up with the wrong answers. Former "Today Show" correspondent Bob Berkowitz has created an "insider's guide" to men: their habits, desires, inspirations, hopes and nightmares.

The Casanova Complex: Compulsive Lovers And Their Woman by Peter Trachtenberg. Pocket Books, New York, 1988. This book was written for men addicted to sex and women addicted to betrayal. It explores the family and cultural dynamics that shape the sexaholic. It is written by a compulsive womanizer and master seducer who intimately defines what it is to be a "love junkie" and identifies the co-dependent women who make it possible.

The Cinderella Complex: Women's Hidden Fear Of Independence by Colette Dowling. Pocket Books, New York, 1981. Some woman are still waiting for "Mr. Right" to transform their lives. This extraordinary book uncovers the roots of women's inner conflicts and shows how all women can achieve a real and lasting liberation.

Making Love Happen by Rebecca Sydnor. British American Publishing, New York, 1989. There is nothing wrong with wanting a satisfying relationship, says Sydnor, a consultant who specializes in romance and courtship in women's lives. Finding a mate is as serious a task as finding a job, yet many women who would never leave their careers to chance, think that love should "just happen." They don't think about what they want in a man or how they should go about getting him. Sydnor offers supportive advice on how to screen out inappropriate men, how to terminate dead-end relationships and how to maintain perspective while dating.

Living Alone And Liking It by Lynn Shahan. Harper & Row, New York, 1981. This is a complete guide to living alone and liking it. Shahan offers valuable and insightful recommendations on coming to terms with loneliness, suddenly being alone (surviving the first few days, weeks and months), venturing out, meeting people, and entertaining guests.

Flirting for Success by Jill Spiegal. MacLester Park Publishers, Minneapolis, 1994.

Chapter Five: *Career and Marriage*

Answers to the Mommy Track by Trudi Ferguson & Joan Dunphy. New Horizon Press, New Jersey, 1991. This is an informative and practical guide which provides specific information every working mother needs to know.

Wall Street Women by Anne B. Fisher. Alfred A. Knopf, New York, 1990. Addresses the issues and concerns of corporate women.

Success and Betrayal: The Crisis of Women in Corporate America by Sarah Hardesty & Nehama Jacobs. Touchstone Books, New York, 1986. This is a must read for the prominent professional business women engaged in today's fast-paced career world.

The Wendy Dilemma: When Women Stop Mothering Their Men by Dan Kiley, PH.D. Avon Publishers, New York, 1984. Kiley offers help to women who want to stop sacrificing themselves by playing mother to the men in their lives.

AUDIO CASSETTES

Adult Children of Divorce. Edward Beal, M.D., and Gloria Hochman. Nightingale-Conant Audio, Chicago, 1991. Hochman, award-winning journalist, and Beal, associate professor of psychiatry, offer healing advice for lasting relationships. This tape focuses on adult children of divorced parents and is designed to help identify patterns and reactions to them.

What Every Woman Ought to Know About Love and Marriage by Joyce Brothers, M.D. Dove Audio, Inc., Beverly Hills, Calif., 1986. One of America's foremost counselors, Brothers offers solid advice on matters every woman wants to know more about and how to get the most from marriage.

The Dance of Anger: A Woman's Guide to Changing the Patterns of Intimate Relationships by Harriet Lerner Goldhor, PH.D. Harper & Row, New York, 1988. Renowned psychologist and psychotherapist Goldhor illustrates how to clarify and change relationships rather than remain stuck in patterns of emotional distancing, or ineffectual fighting and blaming.

Chapter Six: Household Management

Escape from the Kitchen by Denice Schofield. If you are spending too many hours in the kitchen, take advice from Schofield, a home management consultant. Her book will help you to organize your kitchen efficiently and deal with everything from an eight-course dinner party to 357 empty margarine containers!

Bonnie's Household Organizer by Bonnie Runyan McCullough. An essential handbook for the working woman who needs to get her home organized. Each chapter ends with practical suggestions for applying the ideas and techniques to your particular circumstances. Her book also offers suggestions on how to get your husband and children to assist with chores, including a special section on methods for training children to do housework.

Complete Trash by Norman Crampton. Crampton recommends the best, environmentally safe way to discard practically everything around the house.

Clean and Green by Anne Berthold-Bond. A complete guide to non-toxic and environmentally safe housekeeping, this book offers 485 ways in which to clean and disinfect your home without harming yourself, your family, or the environment.

All New Hints From Heloise. A great household guide for the working woman of the '90s. When the "Hints from Heloise" newspaper column was first printed thirty years ago, it was directed toward the housewife. But, today, anyone whose lifestyle demands saving time, money and energy can benefit from reading this book.

Do I Dust or Vacuum? by Don Aslett. Considered the leading authority on house-cleaning, Aslett's home care books are highly recommended. Other titles include *Clutter's Last Stand, Who Says It's a Woman's Job to Clean?* and *Make Your House Do the Work.* His video, *Is There Life After Housework,* is also available through the local library or write: Don Aslett, P.O. Box 1692, Pocatello, ID 83204

Chapter Seven: The Crucial Role of Friendship

Just Friends: The Role Of Friendship In Our Lives by Lillian Rubin. Harper & Row Publishers, New York, 1985. This book will help readers understand themselves and their relationships more fully.

Worlds Of Friendship by Robert Bell. Sage Publications, Beverly Hills, Calif., 1981. Bell supports the importance of emotional ties between women. Some of the topics discussed are meanings of friendship, childhood and adolescent friendships, and women and friendship.

The Givers And The Takers by Cris Evatt and Bruce Feld. Macmillan Publishing Co., New York, 1983. This book helps to explain the emotional aspects of interpersonal relationships by categorizing people into two groups: givers and takers. Contents will help readers come to terms with and, if necessary, alter their "giver" and "taker" traits.

How to Start a Conversation and Make Friends by Don Gabor. Simon & Schuster, New York. This is a great "how-to" guide for breaking the ice.

Women & Friendship by Joel Block, M.D., and Diane Greenberg. Franklin Watts, New York, NY. Block and Greenberg clearly define the dynamics of the female friendship experience.

AUDIO CASSETTES

Coping With Difficult People in Business And Life. Robert Bramson, PH.D. Simon & Schuster, New York, 1986.

Forgiveness Is The Key To Happiness. Gerald Jampolsky, M.D., and Diane Cirincione. Bantam Audio, New York, 1989.

Chapter Eight: **Benefits of a Balanced Diet**

Eat to Win by Dr. Robert Haas. Signet Books, New York, 1983. This book recommends a commonsense diet to increase your energy, strength, speed and endurance. This simple, flexible program explains how to eat for peak fitness, "de-age" your blood in just four weeks and speed healing of sport injuries. It also contains twenty-eight days of menus and 100 peak performance recipes.

You Are What You Eat by Victor Lindlahrs. Lancer Books, New York, 1972. First published in 1940, this book is designed to assist consumers in identifying which foods are non-nutritious and even harmful. It features recommendations on how to prevent illness by eating right, planning balanced meals, and preparing the most beneficial foods.

Vitamin Bible by Earl Mindell. Warner Books, New York, 1985. This definitive book pinpoints which vitamins to take for your particular needs. It also contains updated recommended daily allowances for all vitamins, nutrient therapy for herpes, new heart attack prevention tactics, natural pain killers and the truth about natural anti-aging supplements.

Nutrition Almanac by John Kirschman, Revised Edition. McGraw-Hill Co., New York, 1979. Good nutrition is a prime preventative of illness. Better health can be yours if you know and provide what your body needs.

Sugar Blues by William Dufty. Warner Books, New York. This book highlights the serious hazards of sugar consumption. Although sugar may seem harmless, it is considered a drug and many people are unknowingly addicted.

The Supermarket Handbook by Nikki and David Goldberg. Signet Books, New York, 1976. This invaluable food guide teaches recognition of unnecessary additives harmful to health and provides a listing of the best foods by brand name. It is filled with information about nutritious, whole and natural foods, recipes, and proper use of substitute foods and ingredients.

Dying To Be Thin by Ira Sacker, M.D., and Marc Zimmer, PH.D. Warner Books, New York, 1987. With more than two million anorexics and bulimics in the U.S. today, the numbers are growing to epidemic proportions. Two experts who have helped hundreds of anorexics and bulimics return to healthy lives explain in detail the causes and symptoms of these disorders, and how and where to find help.

Hypoglycemia: A Better Approach by Paavo Airola, PH.D. Health Plus Publishers, Phoenix, Ariz., 1977. On of the world's leading nutritionists offers his suggestions on how to eliminate low blood sugar and improve general health.

This Is Living: How I Found Health and Happiness by Lynn Redgrave. Penguin Books, New York, 1991. Redgrave gives a candid and inspirational account of her lifelong struggle to lose weight and keep it off. She discusses her triumph over dieting with the help of Weight Watchers. About more than weight loss, this book delves into self-acceptance and appreciation, offering solutions to others who struggle with her weight.

Chapter Nine: Benefits of a Good Night's Sleep

Sleeping Problems by Dietrich Langen, M.D. Consolidated Book Publishers, Secaucus, N.J., 1978.

A Good Night's Sleep by Jerrold S. Maxmen, M.D. W.W. Norton & Company, New York, 1981.

Sleep by Quentin Regestein, M.D., and David Ritchie. Consumer Report Books, Mount Vernon, New York, 1990.

Everybody's Guide to Natural Sleep by Philip Goldberg and Daniel Kaufman. Jeremy P. Tarcher, Inc., Los Angeles, Calif., 1990.

The Complete Book of Massage by Clare Maxwell-Hudson. Random House, New York, 1988.

Hands on Healing by the editors of Prevention Magazine Health Books. Rodale Press, Emmaus, PA.

Alternative Healing: The Complete A to Z Guide to Over 160 Different Alternative Therapies by Kastner M. Burroughs, Halcyon Books, New York, 1993.

Chapter Ten: The Art of Self-nurturing

Color

Color With Style by Donna Fujii, Graphic-sha Publishing Co., Tokyo, Japan, 1993. This book is intended to give the reader a background on color and its application.

Showing Your Colors by Jeanne Allen. Chronicle Books, San Francisco, Calif., 1986. The author leads you through a tour of more than one thousand color combinations for your wardrobe.

Color In Fashion: A Guide To Coordinating Fashion Colors by Yoko Ogawa, Junko Yamamoto and Ei Kondo. Rockport Publishers, Mass. A practical, easy-to-use handbook about coordinating colors in fashion.

Fashion & Color by Kojiro Kumagai. Graphic-sha Publishing, Tokyo, Japan. Some color combinations were taboo in the past. By skillfully combining certain colors in the right amounts, almost any color can be used to produce a pleasing effect. Try re-color coordinating your present wardrobe with the use of this book and you will find that you can create more clothing options than you thought were possible.

Camouflaging Figure Problems

The Overnight Guide To Dressing Thin by Mary Martin Niepold. Running Press, Philadelphia, PA. This book will help you to select the right clothes to make you look thinner, whatever your size.

Hot Tips: 1000 Fashion & Beauty Tricks by Frances Patiky Stein. Putnam Publishing, New York. A portable encyclopedia of fashion, beauty and health tips.

The Complete Bonnie August Dress Thin System by Bonnie August. Rawson, Wade Publishers, New York, 1987. When diet isn't the answer, this book will offer you ways to reshape your body with clothes.

Aging

Look Younger, Live Longer by Gayelord Hauser. Farrar, Straus and Co., New York. Sound advice that should make the mature years of life into a healthier and happier time.

A Woman's Best Years by W. Beran Wolfe, M.D. Emerson Books, New York. Written for women who realize that the only way to remain forever young is to grow up, to accept the challenge of maturity, and to enjoy it.

Psychology of Appearance

The Beauty Myth by Naomi Wolf. William Morrow and Co., New York. Exposes the relentless cult of female beauty and the hidden agenda that drives this destructive obsession. Wolf examines the forces that coerce women into participating in their own torture—starving themselves and even submitting their bodies to the knife.

Contact: The First Four Minutes by Leonard Zunin, M.D. and Natalie Zunin. Ballantine/Self Help Books, New York, 1972. Explores the first few minutes of contact and the preconceptions that each person brings to that first meeting.

Dying To Be Thin by Ira M. Sacker, M.D. and Marc A. Zimmer, PH.D. Warner Communications. This book deals with the obsessions of being excessively thin, explaining the causes and symptoms of anorexia and bulimia.

Chapter Eleven: *Setting Goals that Can Change Your Life*

Open Your Mind to Prosperity by Catherine Ponder. Unity Books, Unity Village, MO., 1971. There are many success courses and books available today, but most cover only about one fourth of the formulas given in this book.

Visualization: Directing the Movies in Your Mind by Adelaide Bry. Barnes & Noble Books, New York, 1978. A clear and solid introduction to visualization methods.

Creative Visualization by Shakti Gawain. Bantam Books, New York, 1985. This clear and practical guide with easy-to-follow visualization exercises and affirmations will help you to make dynamic changes in your life.

Creating Money: Keys to Abundance by Sanaya Roman and Duane Packer, P.O. Box 1082, Tiburon, CA 94920. A step-by-step guide to creating money and abundance. These easy-to-learn techniques, positive affirmations and exercises will help you create rapid changes in your prosperity and lead you to mastery over your life.

Getting Organized by Stephanie Winston. Warner Books, New York, 1978. Winston shows you how to be organized in everything from financial planning to meal planning. It is the ultimate in "how-to" books.

The Ninety-Minute Hour by Jay Levinson. E.P. Dutton, New York, 1990. This revolutionary approach to thinking about time targets executives, managers, and anyone else who must balance a heavy work load and illustrates the difference between "working smart" and "working hard."

Think and Grow Rich by Napoleon Hill. Fawcett Crest, New York, 1960. Hill discusses his formula for success...not only what to do, but how to do it.

Unlimited Power by Anthony Robbins. Fawcett Columbine, New York, 1986. How to reprogram your mind in minutes to eliminate fears and phobias, fuel your body with health and energy, improve your interpersonal relationships and much more.

Women and Self-Esteem by Linda Sanford and Mary Ellen Donovan. Penguin Books, New York, 1984. Examines how women's harmful attitudes about themselves are shaped. Offers step-by-step exercises to resolve the dilemma women face in building higher self-esteem.

Self-Esteem by Matthew McKay and Patrick Fanning. St. Martin's Press, New York, 1987. Advice on how to take criticism, how to speak out for what you really need, and how to combat your critical inner voice.

The DO IT Series by James R. Sherman, PH.D. Pathway Books, 700 Parkview Terrace, Golden Valley, MN 55416 (612) 377-1521. Sherman offers a series of highly-recommended, short books, including *Plan For Success, Do It, No More Mistakes* and *Patience Pays Off.*

AUDIO CASSETTES

Anthony Robbins Personal Power Program For Unlimited Success. Guthy-Renker Corp., Robbins Research International, Inc., San Diego, Calif.

Think and Grow Rich. Napoleon Hill. Success Motivation Cassettes, P.O. Box 8018, Waco, TX 76714-8018.

Positive Imaging. Dr. Norman Vincent Peale. Tape Data Media, Inc. 560 S. State College Blvd., Fullerton, CA 92631.

Goal Setting. Barrie Konicov. Potentials Unlimited Inc., 4808-DH Broadmoor S.E., Grand Rapids, MI 49508

VIDEO RECORDING

Self-Esteem and Peak Performance. Jack Canfield. Career Track Publications, 3085 Center Green Dr. Boulder CO 80308-9930.

Chapter Twelve: The Power of Negotiation

You Can Negotiate Anything by Herb Cohen. Lyle Stuart, Inc., Secaucus, N.J., 1980. This book is full of negotiating strategies that can be used for anything from parent and child relationships to complex international dealings. Without becoming mired in technical terminology or legalese, Cohen teaches the win-win approach.

How To Close Every Sale by Joe Girard. Warner Books, New York, 1989. "The world's greatest salesman," Joe Girard, (listed in the Guinness Book of World Records) describes the fundamental principles and crucial fine points that many salespeople overlook.

How To Sell Anything To Anybody by Joe Girard. Warner Books, New York, 1977. Sharp and fascinating reading, this book gives specific techniques in successful selling for both the novice and the experienced salesperson. Over a million copies in print.

More Power To You by Connie Glaser and Barbara Smalley. Warner Books, New York, 1992. Everything you need to know on power communications to command the attention you want. Contains descriptions on how to alter speech patterns, the gestures you use, writing styles, listening skills, and how to ask the right questions.

Thinking Strategically: The Competitive Edge in Business, Politics and Everyday Life by Avinash K. Dixit and Barry J. Nalebuff. W.W. Norton & Co., New York, 1991. Required reading at the best business schools, this book outlines the basics of good strategy making and then tells you how you can apply them to any area of your life.

The Global Edge by Sandra Showdon. Simon and Schuster, New York, 1986. An international guide for business travelers on how to negotiate abroad, this work offers tactics on negotiating in twenty-four major countries.

AUDIO CASSETTES

Getting To Yes: How to Negotiate An Agreement Without Giving In. Roger Fisher. Simon & Schuster Sound Ideas, New York, 1987. Most of us see bargaining as a contest with only winners and losers. Fisher, the director of the Harvard Negotiation Project, shares information on how to negotiate on the merits instead.

Get To The Point: How To Say What You Mean and Get What You Want. Karen Berg and Andrew Gilman. Bantam Audio, New York, 1989. Whether your presentation is a sixty-second, face-to-face encounter with your boss in the elevator, a stint on the witness stand, addressing a group of your co-workers, or a formal presentation to hundreds, this sixty-minute audio program is your guide to authoritative self-expression.

Coping With Difficult People. Robert Bramson, PH.D. Simon & Schuster Sound Ideas, New York, 1986. Bramson, a psychologist and management consultant, instructs on how to remain sane, dignified and optimistic when dealing with even the most difficult people.

How To Use Tact & Skill In Handling People. Paul Parker. Success Motivation Cassettes, P.O. Box 7614, Waco, TX 76714-7614.

How To Get People To Think And Act Favorably With You. Millard Bennett. Success Motivation Cassettes, P.O. Box 7614, Waco, TX 76714-7614.

Sales Power. David Lee. Consciousness Tapes, 2210 Wilshire Blvd., Suite 604, Santa Monica, CA 90403 (213)392-1406. Learn how to achieve sales success and communicate your ideas easily and clearly.

The Survival Guide for Today's Career Woman

by Victoria Rayner

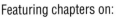

Women have a natural instinct to create meaning in their lives. This book focuses on all aspects of how the professional woman can enjoy her life and career to the fullest.

Written especially for women who want to lead a full life … and are willing to make the extra effort to learn how to do so.

A how-to manual for women who want to stop being victims … and adopt a pro-active plan for a vital and successful lifestyle.

Featuring chapters on:

Career and Marriage	Goal-Setting	Being Single
Friendship	Women in the Workplace	Coping with Stress
Problem-Solving	Nutrition	Negotiation

YES! Please send me ___ copy(s) of *The Survival Guide for Today's Career Woman* by Victoria Rayner at $19.95 per copy plus $2 shipping and handling. Enclosed is my check or money order for $_____ made payable to Info Net Publishing.

Name _____

Address _____

City_____

State and Zip _____

Phone_____

Please send order and funds to:
   phone (714) 489-9292
   fax (714) 489-9595

Info Net Publishing
34188 Coast Highway, Suite C
Dana Point CA 92629